PAY

RICHARD HERZOG

NEWMAN SPRINGS PUBLISHING
320 Broad Street
Red Bank, NJ 07701

First originally published by Newman Springs Publishing 2021

Cover photography and design by David and Richard Herzog.

Some names have been changed to protect potential readers
from incurring any emotional and/or mental distress.

ISBN 978-1-63692-399-4 (Paperback)
ISBN 978-1-63692-400-7 (Hardcover)
ISBN 978-1-63692-401-4 (Digital)

Printed in the United States of America

For those who have experienced and suffered from sexual abuse.

Many thanks to Brent, Matt, and Scotty Goodrich,
David Herzog, Kate Lechler, Carroll McMahan,
Carol Moore, Greg Saucier, and Neil White.

And a very special thank you to my adopted dad, Colby Kullman.

"If a story is in you, it has to come out."

—William Faulkner—

DECEMBER 21, 2000

"It started with a condom box, remember?" I asked. "It was our first year at Archbishop Shaw."

"Yes," Naomi said. "That was a long time ago." We sat across from each other at Joey K's, an uptown hub on Magazine St., six blocks north of the Mississippi River. Rain and dampness had penetrated my bones. Christmas was four days away, but our meeting had placed my yuletide spirit on hold.

"Almost thirty years ago, but barely a whisper for a boy who supposedly had fallen in love for the first time. And there were many first times in our relationship."

"Yes, there were many firsts for both of us."

Jitters had settled in. The same way it did on the flight to my historic hometown—an acrophobic anxiety of being suspended on a wire thousands of feet high with no bar for balance and no net to catch me.

"That's now an old condom box, but it's still as memorable as a newborn baby," I said. I unzipped my coat. Beads of sweat had formed in the middle of my chest.

"Well, yes. I guess," she said. Naomi appeared reserved and reticent. Given the amount of nervous energy which saturated the air, it was understandable. She squeezed her water glass with both hands—hands which had caressed me when I was fifteen. A bolt of pain shot through my veins when I saw her wedding rings, reopening an incurable sore.

Therapists said my scars were permanent, but perhaps one day, peace was possible. It made me wonder how I'd ever achieve closure on the matter. Against the advice of one therapist, I had taken it upon myself to search for her, knowing she would hide and die with the secret. I searched as a person who was offended, trying to come to terms with forgiveness, for her and for myself.

Save for a few wrinkles that had formed around her brow, Naomi looked the same, as elegant as the first time I had seen her and as august as the last time: May 18, 1975. Graduation Day. I walked out of the ceremony, foregoing the traditional cap tossing. My younger brother had followed me to the parking lot, convincing me to take a picture with her—so I could remember those things I should never forget. Since then, I had thought about her daily, without fail.

"Funny how something so small could lead to something so big and life changing," I said. She shot me a quizzical look. "We started as friends, about as friendly as a student–teacher could or should have been. Then it grew as naturally as breathing, something far more profound."

"Yes, it did."

"But along the way, you ignored the influences which drove me to you, or you chose to forget. Then again, maybe you didn't even notice them. Perhaps you were too worried about saving your own skin, too self-absorbed in the aftermath to find me and to see how I was doing."

"Yes, it grew into something much more than I thought it would be," she said. I did my best to stay in the moment, refraining from drinking in her beauty, the very essence of which nearly killed me. I hung on to every word and to her New Orleans accent, which had thickened over time. But time had only been good to one of us.

Time told me to write my story—that of a child whose formative years converged into a storm, a teenager who survived his high school hurricane. A story of a man forever grappling with the notion that a person who supposedly loved him had sexually abused him. A story which shows how abuse occurs upon a young male by the hands of an adult female. Time had presented many questions; time also provided answers.

Part 1

CHAPTER 1

1957 and 1975. How many people, I had wondered, owned identical birth years and high school graduation digits? Was it fate? God sharing a joke? New Orleans voodoo? A Haley's once-in-a-lifetime-comet occurrence? Or just a coincidence?

And what was it like for a child of those numbers to be raised in a sinuous city? Calm winds and hurricanes? Love and anger? Friends and foes? Peace and pain? Simple and complex? Catholic saints and everyday sinners?

I had come to the realization that it was all of these, life on life's terms, a living reflection of my city. Yet, the years '57 to '75 were all part of a purpose driven plan which had driven me to seek shelter in the embrace of a New Orleans lady, which had driven me to seek steps to recovery. The road traveled was littered with more ingredients than seafood gumbo, clothed in a climate known to make or break a person.

My culture was a combination of colliding forces—crawfish boiling in a big, easy pot. The early years were a rat's maze, hitting a wall at every turn, bouncing in and out of my home, school, and the neighborhood. Mix in my appetite for the opposite gender with my desire to be loved, and the result was a crazy Cajun child reeling on a roller coaster ride. But sometimes, the ride was cushioned by summer swims, sports, movies, music, and bike rides. And my teacher named Naomi.

The culture had a pulse named New Orleans, my "city that care forgot." A carefree spirit where my weekend was longer than my work week. Louis Armstrong's and Pete Fountain's musical spirit

11

ran through my veins—a local "who dat and where ya at" who lived to drink and eat but rarely in that order. I loved beaucoup booze and food: beer, bourbon, and rum on the liquid side; crawfish, file gumbo, and dressed po'boys on the solid side. I was a saint and a sinner who ran the fields with the same gusto as I had run to the bars.

But I watched others die while living out our New Orleans mantra: *Laissez les bon temps rouler*. Let the good times roll. Roll with the Big Muddy river, not a care in the world. Eventually, I learned that ecstasy exacts a price when I attended funerals of those gone too soon, waving a handkerchief in the wind, while strutting the second line. Folks simply took it all in stride, claiming c'est la vie.

Years after Naomi, I had to decide if the pleasure was worth the pain, because some pain can be too hard to take; some pain can take too long from which to recover and learn. I had to choose to stay or give up the two leading ladies in my life at the end of the '57–'75 years: the teacher and the city. Thirty, forty, fifty or more years down the road, I'd come to miss only one of the two.

*****

Just prior to midnight in March of 1957, a doctor slapped my backside and welcomed me to the *Crescent City*. No pictures; not then and few after we left Touro Infirmary, a hospital near the intersection of Prytania and Louisiana Avenues. Photos required spending, and when I arrived as child number five, money was in high demand and in short supply.

Placed in the arms of my parents, I was shipped on the Jackson Avenue Ferry, where over the AM airwaves, it was announced that Admiral Richard Byrd had died. Before the boat docked, I was given his first name. To this day, my resemblance to the Navy explorer is more extreme than the North and South Poles. My mind, body, and spirit continue to reside at the equator. As the car traveled down the ferry ramp, my mom welcomed me to Gretna—the city where I lived for eighteen years and then some. I didn't listen to her then, nor during the many years which followed.

The only cultural difference between New Orleans and Gretna, where our rental house resided, was the spelling. The only distance between the two was the river. Not everyone could afford or fit in New Orleans—a town surrounded by bayous, canals, and lakes. People sought land and opportunity where they could and took the Southern Louisiana lifestyle with them.

While neither one of my husbandless grandmothers lived in Gretna when I was born, people said the person I most resembled was my great-uncle Willie. Uncle to my mom, he had an unparalleled sense of humor and an interesting perspective on life. And he did things his own, eccentric way. Each Christmas, he decorated his television with assorted bells and bows and a chain secured with a padlock—"so no one would steal the goddamn thing."

I also inherited his work ethic. Part of his cash flow was derived from rowing a skiff loaded with banana bushels. Paddling started at sunrise, pushing away from the Gretna levee, and struggling against perilous waters toward the New Orleans side. He rowed until the sun set behind the big bend upriver. Lore stated six-foot-four-inch Willie could "cut a rug" and wasted no time dancing upon the heads of anyone who tested him. The police refused to enter a bar whenever he was involved. And he never lost a fight.

Save for a few inches in height, I additionally inherited his penchant for fighting, and I only fought when provoked. And life at the Herzog house presented daily opportunities: fight for a seat at the table; fight for food. Fight to use the one bathroom; fight to hold it in. Fight for floor furnace space; fight from the heat of the belt. Fight with my parents; fight with the neighbors. Watch parents fight each other; watch them fight the neighbors. Never was noise far away. Uncle Willie's DNA, combined with my environment, set the wheels in motion for a roller coaster ride nothing short of erratic.

Bob and Barbara Pearl Herzog carried across the water on March 11 more than their Richard "Roux, Roux," a nickname I still acknowledge. They carried memories of loved ones buried at a young age, the remnants of two world wars and the Great Depression. They carried the past, the present, and a foggy future—which, over the years, defined their angst, simplicity, and tenacity. Less than two years later, they carried Thomas, the youngest. He joined me and siblings Bill, Bobby, David, and Mary in a house which felt no larger than a sewing machine box.

CHAPTER 2

Eight people. Eight hundred square feet. Our 528½ Madison Street house rested on frail cinder blocks and in the shadow of a two-story apartment filled with three occupants. Helen the hen, who resembled a barnyard fowl, was the neighborhood watchdog. Her chain-smoking, curmudgeon husband, Slim, was flagpole tall and wide. Both were the bottom dwellers, sucking up garbage when it landed around them.

Ms. Quinn, the landlord, inhabited the top. A beanstalk replica of Slim, she seldom washed her hair and seemed to have worn the same clothes for days on end. Although obsessively protective of her junk, Ms. Quinn let kids be kids, always staying above the neighborhood fray.

I'd work up the courage to knock on her door and ask permission to use a can and a brush to paint images on the sidewalk. I would search among dusty dishes, soiled mattresses, broken televisions, dirty windows, yesterday's newspapers, commodes filled with books and plungers, and too much to recall. New York's Collyer brothers paled by comparison. The only things missing were corpses and coffins and my mother, who would have died on the spot had she toured Ms. Quinn's museum.

If there were a more paradoxical pair on planet earth than my mom and all things Quinn, I never met them. If the scales in our house tipped to the dirty, my mom let the neighborhood know it. "Goddamnsonofabitchandbastard" was her favorite cuss word, an anathema strung together as a warning shot signifying an announcement loomed. "How many goddamn times do I have to tell y'all to pick up your damn clothes? And it better goddamn be done before we leave for church!" Spiritual vulgarity.

I never failed to ask her where on heaven's earth did she want us to put the clothes. It helped little that she was a compulsive cleaner, inside and outside the house, the soul included. Her cleaning trait stuck with me into adulthood, minus the spiritual vulgarity.

"In your drawer would be a good place to start! Where the hell else would you put 'em?" she'd answer.

One dresser draw. Five boys with a ten-year span from youngest to oldest shared a single bedroom, while my parents slept in the other. My curly, blonde-haired sister, Mary, slept in the "living room" the size of a shirt button. Our laundry piled higher than a Louisiana landfill, and I would have gladly given one of my two pairs of socks, pants, and shirts away to have provided more room. And to keep from hearing my mom fuss and cuss.

8 people. 8 hundred square feet. 528 ½ Madison St.

As much as she hated asking, my mom sometimes borrowed landlord Quinn's motorized wringer washer, save for days she had hung our diapers over the tub after dipping them into the commode. Wringer linen hung from clothesline pins; sheets and shirts and such blew with the wind's rhythm, as we played chase in and around them.

We once thought we'd pin baby Tommy to the line. He was spaghetti thin and had inherited Herzog ears—perfect for pin attachments. It helped little that nobody heard his screams when he ran his arm through the wringer, hung out to dry in the apartment shed littered with tools, car parts, and flat bike tires covered with spiderwebs. It helped less that our dad's income fell far too short to purchase appliances. I guessed he had stashed a few pennies aside to buy Dixie longnecks brewed on Tulane Avenue.

"Dat won't hurt him," he once said. Dad was tighter than Tommy's wringer arm when he had shared his beer with our pup, Snoopy. I watched Snoop lap up the liquid, walk laps around the bowl, then collapse into a snooze. Fear gripped my heart thinking he had died, until I noticed the rise and fall of his belly. Two weeks later, I cried myself to sleep, after having watched a city bus roll over him.

Much to her chagrin, Barbara Pearl Perrett never liked a beer nor a dog she met. And in New Orleans, there were more corner bars than bus stops. Except for cooking, my mom seemed to have liked little of anything. Including one of her parents.

"I don't like him at all!" she once told my aunt. They were sister-in-laws who shared the same first name.

"But we are called to love one another, Barbie," she replied. My aunt Barbara, who revealed this to me five years after my mom passed away, said she and my mom had been teenagers at the time.

"How can I love him when I don't even like him?" my mother asked. Like my sister, Mom was railroad track thin. Her hazel eyes complemented her blonde hair. Photos captured her at a young age—locks sitting upon her shoulders supported by her five-foot-five-inch frame.

"Jesus, Barbie! This is your dad!" Aunt Barbara said.

"Yes. This *is my* dad, who lives somewhere else and brings other women to our house! Whether my mom is there or not. I don't ever want to be known as a Perrett."

*****

The first time I met Grandpa Perrett, I didn't like him either. He was in a drunken stupor. He swayed near the front door of my Maw-Maw's second floor government housing project, one of several scattered around low-income areas in New Orleans. Grandpa was too bent over to be the six-foot-four-inch man Uncle Willie once described. A cigarette habit had stained his fingers and had plastered yellow paint onto his teeth; the color of his jacket meshed with both and drooped over his shoulders. I didn't like what I heard, either.

"Get out! Get out, you son of a bitch! Get away from the children!" Maw-Maw screamed. She landed solid broom blows against his torn fedora and unshaven face.

My Maw-Maw was my closest grandparent. We shared the same birthday and a thousand laughs. She fed and clothed me and never beat me over the head with religion, nor a broom. Her home was one of my favorite places. The smell of red beans and coffee and nighttime opened windows kept me safe and secure, even when sirens wailed in the distance—the men in blue chasing down drunks causing domestic quarrels.

But in Grandpa's drunken moment, I felt the walls cracking, as I sat crouching under the kitchen table, scared shitless. I had a full view of his socks protruding from his boots and a view of my uncle Clay heading upstairs to get his .38 revolver. It was the same weapon he strapped to his hip when he pulled federal building security duty, the trade he learned during World War II. A gun and a broom. My only living grandad was soon to be shot and swept into the stairwell.

Years down the road, I came to love Grandpa only half as much as I disliked him. A flame burned in my heart after I learned his history. Some folks said he was a well-liked, intelligent man, who took little seriously, except women and the bottle. Others said he was a different father and spouse after he returned from killing Austro Hungarian belligerents during World War I; he had grown worse after his twenty-one-year-old son preceded him in death. Robert Junior's neck had snapped like a twig in a hurricane, when he dove into a shallow Missouri lake.

*****

While I had the charismatic character of Uncle Willie, my uncle Clay, Maw-Maw's living son, was closest to my heart. He taught me the meaning of giving, often sliding cash or purchasing gifts for me and my siblings. He cared enough to pull the trigger had Grandpa put a finger on us. And he loved the New Orleans Saints enough that, in 1969, he bought me and my siblings' season tickets, but he never attended a game. His eyesight prevented him from purchasing a seat in Tulane stadium.

But Uncle Clay, like myself, had a front row seat to his role model dad and wars, domestic and overseas. Genes and New Orleans can be more powerful than the mind. And like Robert Senior and many veterans, Uncle Clay became a binge drinker going on two-week, nonstop stretches while Maw-Maw lay awake, waiting to catch and release verbal hell when he returned home.

It helped little Uncle Clay could barely see sober and see nothing while under the influence, particularly his wallet when bartenders and cabdrivers robbed him blind. When I earned my driver's license at seventeen, he'd drop a dime in the pay phone, asking me to come pick him up from a local bar. It was one way to stop the thieves from stealing his money. As I watched him stumble to their front door, I prayed he'd never put a hand on Maw-Maw. It would never have been a question of whom to defend, but a matter of how I would have lived with myself for having hurt Uncle Clay.

On my ride home, I thought how it might have been better if some men like Uncle Clay and Grandpa would have been better off dying in war—rather than coming home to fight life's battles.

*****

"We gonna putcha right chere, Mr. Robert. Sunshine sho do ya some good," a Louisiana State Hospital orderly said. I remember him guiding Grandpa's wheelchair onto a patio attached to a building once known as the State Insane Asylum. I was uncertain how I had drawn the unlucky straw to visit Grandpa in such an environment, but something told me Bob and Barbara wanted to keep an eye on their "trouble child."

Grandpa was a zombie the second time we had come face-to-face. He was more hunchbacked bent, and he owned kerosene breath. A frightening, faraway look spoke from his eyes. His words were inaudible, and he coughed more than he spoke. The orderly wiped Grandpa's mouth each time saliva dripped onto his garments.

"Why is he just lying there?" I asked. It was the third and final time I had seen him. Grandpa was clean shaven, wore a suit, and had nothing to say, stretched straight in a flag-draped casket.

"He's asleep," my dad answered.

"Well, wake him up."

"It's da kinda sleep you don't wake up from."

I looked at my dad, then looked at Grandpa, never under-standing my first sight of a dead man. My dad held to my shoulder. Human touch was something that rarely occurred for me as a child, but I remember how in an instant it made everything right in the world. Until I heard the cries around me. I joined them, because my mother cried uncontrollably. I was afraid she might fall asleep, too.

It helped little that she never had the dad she wanted and that her brother's death had come on the heels of the Great Depression—which, in subsequent years, became synonymous with my mom's mental disposition. Daily demons haunted her. She stayed close to the shore and closer to home, never venturing away, even when Hurricane

Betsy blew hell upon the city. The sound of a hundred locomotives howled through the bridge barriers. The same Greater New Orleans Bridge, which incited near heart failure whenever she was forced to drive across, and damn near killed anyone riding with her.

Every day was a roller coaster ride: a slow, steady rise to the top, a furious freefall into forever.

CHAPTER 3

I was a crayon crammed in a box—an individual color, marking memories to the paint by number orders doled out by my mother—a heavy hand who ruled with a leather strap—her way or the beltway. She eventually discovered one of her crayons to have been wrapped a tad tighter than his siblings, and that crayon craved to get out of the box.

"You've been running the trains again?" she asked. Her voice cracked during most inquisitions. I stood at the top of our house steps, looking up through a screen door at a face which mirrored a priest in a confessional. "I said, 'Have you been running the trains again?'"

"Riding?" I asked. I was afraid to answer a question with a question. Fearful to ask anything, since she wanted to control every thought and move I made. Riding was within the realm of possibility, since I'd sometimes jump the train, which motored down the center of Madison Street. Riding was certainly more dangerous but less conspicuous than running a strand of stationary boxcars perfectly parked and aligned with Ms. Quinn's apartment.

"I said, 'R-U-N-N-I-N-G!'" she screamed.

"No, ma'am."

"Like hell! Mrs. Hazel saw you!"

"Then why did you ask if you knew the answer?"

I wanted to yell "goddamnsonofabitchandbastard" each time the belt made its mark but abstained fearing it would incite further affliction—landing soap in my mouth. I was still spitting suds from a bar the week prior.

Fight or flight strengthened my resolve and will. My mom talked up religion and threatened to beat the hell out of me—all in the same sentence. My head emerged thick as a brick, a mind too young to understand the meaning of a double standard. What she missed was a child crying out to be loved, a boy who sought refuge and assurance that all was going to be all right, even if it wasn't.

Even while I was living in the middle of it, I was too young to comprehend her history: an alcoholic father who was an infantryman, a brother who had accidentally died at age twenty-one, a brother who served in a war, her future spouse who fought in that war and who eventually worked all day as she battled depression, while raising six children in a space in which I could spit from one end to the other. I surmise my inability to listen and to conform only added fuel to the fire.

"Go to your room and get your project done!" She had issued another marching order.

"But today is Friday, and it's not due until Monday," I said. "Can't I watch TV with everyone else?"

"Hell no! And God will punish you if you disobey me!"

"So, I get punished twice? First by you and then by him?"

"You're damn right!"

"Please, can I watch TV?" She sent one of her "I'm getting ready to whip your ass" looks.

The family sat watching *Amos and Andy* with *The Andy Griffith Show* on deck. Mary sat in my dad's lap, while the boys were spread across the floor, unless they had fought for and won a piece of the couch. Everyone's eyes were glued to the three-channeled television.

All but one who walked to solitary confinement with paper and pencils, forced to make Columbus's three ships seaworthy. Their laughter was a distraction for an agitated artist, who voiced his displeasure at every chance. During commercials, parental visits ensued with a repetitive directive: shut up and draw or you'll be kneeling on rice while praying the rosary. Moments like these, which had accumulated over time, drove me to seek solace in vices readily available in New Orleans culture.

Drawing, however, was more appealing than reciting the rosary, a string of beads used to count Catholic prayers: *The Our Father, The Hail Mary* and *The Glory Be,* or as I dubbed it, the glory beads. Along with beans and pralines, beads were a prominent part of our lives, especially as they related to Catholicism.

The Hail Marys consisted of five sets. Each set had ten beads and was preceded by an *Our Father.* I reduced *The Hail Marys* to five per set by grabbing two beads at a time—a method I called "killing two prayers in one tone."

"Okay, Dad. I'm finished. Come see the drawings," I said. My call once again disrupted their black and white comedy, but the chance to upset them seemed pleasurable. When he entered, I sunk *La Nina, Pinta*, and *Santa Maria* and all the stickmen on board, tearing each sheet in half. He locked the door, then he tore into me.

His bullwhip belt met my skin with an authoritative fury. I weaved and bobbed, jabbed and grabbed, and landed nothing but air. I dropped and rolled, burned by the leather, as my skin seemed to have shed from my bones. My hand reached for a doorknob; my ribs extended to a whipping post position. I detected death in the near distance.

My siblings made their way through a backdoor and fought him until he quit. My sister cried, kneeling in a corner, hands clasped, her *Hail Mary* murmuring above the stop of the storm. No sleep came that night. I lay awake burning in pain, recalling a family who lived across from the church and how their dad beat them, forcing them to lie on the floor, legs up and tied together, while the belt and buckle scorched their feet.

"Jesus, Barbara. By the looks of it, that's the worst beating I've ever seen," the doctor said two days later. He swabbed the cuts and welts. Mom stood with a stare, seeing how one of her six children had not been this discolored since passing through her birth canal.

"I told him I'd leave with the kids if it ever happened again," she said.

It was her first admission that her husband had crossed the line, but it was not the first time I had heard her say she would leave him. I sat listening to them, knowing it would be a long time before I'd look at my dad as my father. But it was a short time before the hot seat got hotter.

"Are you in trouble, again?" Mom asked. Friday after school detention had become routine, so did her lack of patience, made evident by her scowl when she arrived at school.

"Honestly, Mom. I didn't do anything! The teacher gave me detention, because I got a D on my report card."

"All the more reason to punish you." With each stroke, she was determined to get an explanation. I hated my teacher each time the belt tore across my bare bottom.

Teachers said paying attention was difficult for me, that my attention span was no longer than an eraser. Most of my academic issues stemmed from boredom and being under-challenged. And from having a steady eye on the playground and Renee, the cutest girl in my grammar school world who sat two seats away.

*****

Some truths were encouraged to never be spoken in my family. Don't tell this; don't tell that were promises spoken in a whisper to spare anyone pain and retribution. I learned early in life how to hide things—the way Uncle Clay hid the fact he was married while overseas. Questions provoked my curiosity, but I refused to ask, nor was I allowed. My job was to march to the answers I'd been given.

If I wanted information concerning my parents, I simply needed to recall what was said during their arguments, especially when my dad drank. When the tone reached volcanic proportions, evidence emerged.

"Look, woman. I done told you I was sorry. Can't you forget it?" my dad said. "It" raised my kid curiosity. "It" had itched more than a hundred hives, begging to be scratched, until I had been cured by an answer.

"But you didn't tell *me!* You know how I found out," Mom said.

"Yes. We both know dat, and dat was never to be spoken by him." Some truths were revealed in a Catholic Confessional Box—

where a person's transgressions were to be sealed between a priest and God.

"Where are you going?" she asked.

"Men's Club."

"Oh sure!" Her voice had quivered, and her body had swayed, the same way Grandpa did when he was drunk.

"What da hell you mean, 'oh sure?' Where the hell you think I'm going?" Dad tugged his pants when he became flustered. I once thought had he tugged any higher, he'd choke to death and so would their arguing.

"You're going to get tanked up! That's where you're going, god-damnit! Don't you come back here like that, Robbie!"

Men's Club was one of our St. Anthony Grammar School fund-raisers. Men met the first Tuesday of each month throughout the school year. One dollar bought one ticket, and one winning ticket yielded five hundred dollars. One of my brothers struck gold near midnight on a February night. Bobby's dollar came from Maw-Maw, and she gave him the liberty to spend the winnings.

Bobby and I were as different as an atheist and a Catholic. Athletically, we were several football fields apart, since I was the "runner" and the most naturally gifted ball player in the family. He was naturally selfish, and I loathed it. He wallowed in the cash, spending every dime on himself: a black bike with a newspaper basket; model airplanes, battleships, and destroyers. I never got to bomb the ships, play imaginary war at sea, nor ride the bike. His possessions were forbidden and temporary, and his selfishness was permanent.

I never understood "Bobby Black Sheep," as he was sometimes called, no more than I could fathom gambling as an educational moneymaker. Nor could I comprehend boyish men who drank until the clock struck twelve. And even less could I discern my father's "it," though arrows pointed to another woman.

It helped little to recall the images of my mother sitting at the kitchen table, staring into space, her glasses on the table, eyes red and swollen—married to a man with her dad's first name. Her shoulders sagged by the world's weight. Her weeping slid like a Passover angel under my bedroom door.

*****

While life on Madison Street mirrored continuous chaos, I was able to take refuge in other places and with other people, Shepherds who shaped me. If there were one redeeming quality of Catholicism, it was large families, which provided respites and memories with more cousins than I could count.

I labeled it the arms and leg race, a procreation explosion. There was nothing cold in the post-World War II bedroom. Noncontraceptive Catholics had borne children at a rapid pace. In our family, my Aunt Flo had four. Aunt Geri waved the white flag at five. My mother stopped at six after a miscarriage. Aunt Barbara and Aunt Evelyn both birthed eight—an even four boys and four girls. Aunt Lois outran all of them to the finish line with nine.

My aunts were courageous caretakers, all lockstep in their faith and principles. Simple housewives with life's most difficult job. They believed and shared in the golden rule: go outside and stay outside until it was time to eat. Hide under the house if a thunderstorm erupts, which during a New Orleans summer, was as certain as partying. No excuses. In many ways, my aunts influenced me, and they let the crayon out of his box—free to color his world, no matter what I faced. And I knew where they colored the line in their sand, and I had better not cross it.

And their children were equally pivotal. We grew up together: biking, picnics, swimming, Gretna Recreation, American Legion and Catholicism, to name a few. We were children playing in the fields of summer and flocked together at my maternal grandmother's house where she had placed five dollars inside our cards taped to the Christmas tree. I felt safe with them, staying in their homes and with the attention they provided, but caution and care were sometimes thrown to a hurricane.

"Not it!"

"Not it!"

"Not it!" my cousins and my brother David shouted one after the other. It had the sound of an *ack-ack* gun shooting at enemy aircraft.

"Richard's it!" They teased and pointed fingers. I stood dumbfounded, as they buckshot to familiar hiding places.

Cousins Kerry, Larry, Greg, Pat, Lenny, Lucien, George, David and neighbors rounded out the Hide-and-Go-Seek game. We were always on the run playing baseball, football, Not It, and war games. With our baseball bats used as rifles and our *Longest Day* sound effects, battles were intense and usually brought to a cease-fire over who shot whom, who played dead and which nationality was victorious. Sometimes, it depended on where we stood when the bullets stopped flying.

Sunken in St. Augustine Grass

Nearby houses in my cousins' part of Gretna were bigger and better furnished—manicured yards requiring mandatory boundaries. The lone exception was my cousins, a quasi-Herzog house duplicate but with one more bedroom and no landlord. Since the neighborhood was familiar, and I was the fastest, finding then tagging everyone would be easy. I was confident bordering on cocky when I found myself in taboo territory.

The Wilson's partially fenced yard was diagonal to my cousin's. Their home was occupied by a former Army sergeant turned railroad man who loved domestic chores. He was married to a doting, disciplinarian lady and who kept a tighter leash on her three sons than she did on their large animal.

"Run! Take cover! The dog is out! Everybody, run! Everybody..."

Everyone emerged from their hiding places to seek safer shelter. All but me, the "it" boy, and a punk who had spent time at the Wilson's. He was the neighborhood troublemaker, a bucked teeth agitator with a devil's disposition who walked alongside a German shepherd. A block away, Stevie stopped and pointed the dog directly at me. For someone who was the fastest, I stood paralyzed, sunken in St. Augustine grass.

A certain beauty resembled Duke, running scalded in slow motion with upright ears and hair brushed by the wind. Yet he covered ground at the speed of which our family doctor said, "It's a boy!" The dog leaped; his sharp, white fangs were displayed, and saliva had flown from his mouth. He tore into me the way tornado's tear trailer parks, the way a furious father closed a child's opened skin, and opened that which was closed. I pushed and punched and wailed. In a ditch, David stood throwing rocks at Duke, until the dog turned tail and took a piece of his leg, too.

Duke heeled at his owner's command. Mr. Wilson scooped me from the ground. A red hole the length and width of my middle finger caught my eye; flesh and meat dangled down my leg.

"Jesus, Del, what the hell happened?" my aunt asked. She ran alongside a flock of crying cousins who had greeted me on the road. Mr. Wilson looked like a shepherd carrying a lost sheep.

"Damn dog jumped the fence while I was washing the car, Barbara!"

CHAPTER 4

His legs had hung three hundred feet above the Mississippi River, center of a cantilever bridge. He held onto the steel girder. Perhaps when he felt called, he looked over his shoulder at a priest. Local television crews had positioned their cameras, ready to film for the evening news. East and westbound traffic had been halted, but my mind was running in an anticipation fast lane.

I realized how trauma could appear with the same suddenness of a dog jumping a fence or a belt unleashing terror across my body. Both events replayed in reruns. The belt would become a daily visitor to my naked skin, and the dog awakened from the shadows, whenever we marched by during our war games—barking while tearing his teeth into the Wilson's wired fence. They eventually donated Duke as a K-9.

"Poor guys gonna miss red beans and rice," I said.

"That's cold, bra," Perry said. Red beans and rice were close to my stomach but closer to my heart. The delicacy was a New Orleans, Monday tradition, dating back to the nineteenth century when housewives did laundry by hand. Beans cooked for hours while moms slaved cleaning and washing. Pile all the dirty linen from both Barbara's and my aunts, and no one could see the sun set.

Perry and I sat on the edge of a railroad bridge, which provided a train pathway from the levee to the Perry St. Wharf. He was my closest ally in a neighborhood flooded with older boys, an army with a wide range of personalities. Perry and his brother Walton, along with their mother Paisley, moved from Oklahoma, leaving behind an abusive, drunken dad and spouse. All three carried their suitcases a long way, but they never unpacked their baggage. We had much in common.

"Before you came here, I had the name Perry placed on the wharf in those big, black letters, as you can see. Had a street named after you, too," I said. He laughed and enjoyed the compliment, each time I talked about the wharf.

"Why do you think he wants to jump?" he asked. Perry habitually pushed his glasses to his nose brim; I gathered that his eyesight was no better than my uncle Clay's. The March winds struggled to blow his wooly, black hair. Spring had begun, and my birthday was two weeks behind me. No cake. No candle. No photos. But I felt rich with the two dollars Maw-Maw had placed in a card, both stashed in a closet corner. I wanted to give the money to the man sitting on the bridge, if his life had been that bad.

"Not sure he wants to jump. Or die. Maybe he doesn't want to live anymore. My mom says that a lot; says she gets tired of living. I keep wondering if she's gonna die soon," I said.

"My mom's like that. She cries a lot," Perry shared.

"Yep. I gotta tell ya, bro, I hear your mom crying. I sometimes sit under your window, so I can get away from my mom's crying or screaming. You can probably hear her with our windows down."

"Maybe that guy cries a lot. Think he'll do it?" Perry asked.

"If you're crazy enough to get on that rail, then you're crazy enough to jump," I said.

Multitudes pushed toward the levee, mirroring last month's rush to the Mardi Gras River Parade. Navy cruisers, Coast Guard cutters, tugboats, ferry boats, and fireboats floated up and down the Mississippi; flags flew against a February wind. Not this day. Only rescue boats awaited, their engines idling against a murky current.

Perry and I worked our way to the front of the masses. Some had brought beer. Some handed out popsicles. Some yelled for the man to jump. *What if he can hear them? What if he hits a boat instead of the water?* I cringed at the thought and the visual of his skin and bones disintegrating in the light of day, blood and guts scattering across the bow. But there I stood with the rest of them, witnesses at a self-execution. An hour passed. Then two. A helicopter circled the scene. Red beans and rice were calling.

I walked away with my back to the sun and shadowboxed. Perry threw shells which collided with the wind. By the time I returned to Madison Street, the suspense had dulled into its fourth hour. A final look beckoned. He jumped—a flashing figure against the city skyline, a silhouette planted in my nightmares. The six o'clock news showed him surfacing, waving his arms. Until he was scooped from the river, like a Mississippi catfish.

"Where you been at?" I had recognized his loud, unmistakable voice. Perry's bully brother, Walton.

"On the river," Perry said.

"Dumb ass! Didn't I tell you to never go up there without me?"

"No, Walton! I mean, don't…" A solid right landed on Perry's face. His cheeks rippled across the side of his head when Walton's fists met Perry's jaws. He pulled Perry's hair, yanked him into the ditch, and then took to kicking and stomping when his arms had tired. My friend begged and screamed and covered up in what the neighborhood boys called the pussy position.

"Stop crying, you stupid little bastard, or I'll kick the shit out of you!"

"Come on, Walton!" I yelled.

"You want some of this, too?"

I remained quiet, but I held no fear of six-foot-three-inch Walton. He never attacked me the other times I pleaded on Perry's behalf. I was safe knowing David stood at my side. Some of the older boys arrived. Walton backed off. Perry sprinted until their slammed door silenced his wailing. I picked up his glasses. The red beans didn't taste the same that day.

When the dust settled, Walton went home, too. The sun rose the next day, and we played as though nothing had happened. Except for Walton. He stayed inside for days, perhaps embarrassed, perhaps sunken under his bedsheets wondering why his dad had used him as a punching bag. No explanation and no remorse.

In time, Perry physically healed, until the next beating. Walton grew worse trying to determine why he was in this world, like the man who sat swinging his legs above a captive audience. Twenty-eight years after receiving his high school diploma, Walton jumped in the middle of the night. No rescue boats and no six o'clock replay.

*****

"Richard!" my mom screamed. She summoned me from a rectangular window, which opened like a door. It was her usual way to locate me, whether I waited for a man to jump from a bridge, or I was playing with the neighborhood gang.

Shortly after Hurricane Betsy left us waterless and without electricity, we moved thirty feet to a house separated by a patch of grass. The new address faced south and came equipped with one more bedroom, a screened porch, a tin shed, more of Ms. Quinn's garbage and fancy, front windows.

"Richard!" she yelled. I made her holler twice, since we were in the middle of another touch football game. Making her wait provided me the time to run or acknowledge her. With near-death experiences at the turn of every corner, running had become a viable option.

"Yes, ma'am?" I answered.

"The church secretary is on the phone. They want you to serve a funeral!" The church often called, and I rarely refused. Being an altar boy was a dubious honor, an unwritten law upheld by all young males in our Catholic families. It was expected, but many of us left or were forced out after we had "given it a try."

For me, it was all about the perks: free wine and the annual picnic at St. Ben's Seminary—a cloistered abbey insulated by whispering forest pines and the pristine Bogue Falaya River. The "Bogue" was a clay carpet which stuck between our toes, faces, and chests when mud fights erupted.

"Damn! Okay! Tell them I'm coming!"

"Come on, bra. You can't leave now," Greg said. He was one of the older boys who owned a '57 Chevy, which rested on blocks more than it raced.

"You kiddin' me, Herzy? You've been doing this a lot lately," Gary said. He was the other "G" boy, same age as Greg and was gun barrel thin. Gary marched to the tune of his own guitar strum. He introduced me to a few chords while instructing me the technique of pipe smoking. Gary and Greg had influential power; both were Vietnam draft candidates and reminded me how I was a "Miss Goody Two-shoes"—tied too tight to the knot of my mother's apron.

I placed the ball at the line of scrimmage, a long crack in the concrete which ran from ditch to ditch, when someone hollered "river," a clear-the-road warning.

"I got oranges! I got apples! I got melons! I got bananas!" A toothless man, whose rusted wrinkles competed with those of the truck, sang in harmony with the engine. His words hovered above the fumes and the verbal barrage.

"Shithead! Pussy! Woos! Suck up! Go serve your little massy assy your mom wants you to! Why are you so obsessed with death? Jesus!" Their comments struck a nerve: God. Life. Dog mauling. Suicide attempt. Home. Neighborhood. Their words were an angry batch of bees chasing me down the street, until I ran past the corner store to my least favorite ride. Running to a funeral, because I could not stop.

*****

No noise interrupted the black limousine. The priest occupied the rear seat, while I sunk into a reversible one. It reminded me of the kind on the St. Charles Avenue streetcars. We passed canals and shotgun houses, rectangular residences with rooms arranged one behind the other. Locals stated if a person blasted a shotgun from the front door to the backdoor, the pellets could fly and nary touch a wall.

The limo frontside funeral flag flapped in the dead wind. My eyes connected with the chauffeur when he peaked in the rearview mirror. I clutched the larger-than-life size crucifix which had rested between my cassock garments, feeling safer knowing Jesus was along for the ride. I chewed a piece of gum to hide the sacristy wine I hit before adorning my altar garb. A taste on the tongue tamed my nerves, because I could not stop from thinking about the deceased. A he? A she? Young? Old? I never asked the priest. In my own strange way, I wanted it to be a surprise.

Mothe Funeral Home was a family owned, plantation structure catty-corner to St. Bart's and St. Mary's cemeteries. Azaleas circled the perimeter. Pine and Cypress trees shaded the façade. We were ushered inside by a man in a suit to die for and directed to the parlor where family and friends awaited. Only the swishing of our holy garments could be heard when the gathered parted, paving a path to the dais. A trail of tears had followed our footsteps.

A transformed figure of somebody's someone lay beneath us— an elderly man with blue scabs scattered on a scalp partially covered with hair strands. His hands appeared older than his face, a sunken, embalmed visage shy of a century. A rosary snaked through his fingers. I stood as still as he lay, petrified by the finality of life, and wondered if he was burning in hell or tossing footballs in heaven.

"The Lord is my shepherd...he restores my soul," the priest said. He had read Psalm 23 perfunctorily, breathed between verses, while resting a prayer book on his belly.

A line formed to kiss their loved one good-bye. I struggled to still the crucifix. The mourning reached a crescendo, as an employee closed the casket lid; the elderly's face was forever gone.

Hook and Ladder Cemetery was surrounded by white walls and wrought iron gates. Sun-soaked tombs stretched shadows across Faith, Hope, and Love lanes. Love was my favorite. Names and dates occupied the marble plaques and headstones. I searched for one, which shared my birthday.

"Father? Why are the graves above ground?" After repeated funerals, I had finally worked up the nerve to ask.

"Well, New Orleans and its surrounding areas are below sea level. Which means the water table is high," he said. His array sparkled in the afternoon sun. I felt important, leading the procession in the company of priestly power.

"I don't understand."

"If you place a casket in the ground, one bad storm could cause it to float away. Sometimes, the lid tends to open, which usually results in a body floating down a street." I shook my head, knowing I lived in Float City—Mardi Gras floats, boats afloat, caskets and bodies afloat.

"How can so many people be buried in one grave?" I asked.

"Grave workers remove the most recent coffin and place the remains at the rear of the vault. Then they destroy the removed coffin. This makes room for the next deceased."

I decided to stop asking questions; the unknown and the answers provoked fear. It had driven me from a football game to something darker, as though I was drawn to things and people I should have run from.

No further than a stone's throw, church bells rang. Pallbearers slid the coffin into the tomb. "Even though I walk through the valley of the shadow of death…" I faintly heard the priest say. My mind drifted to moments during 6:15 a.m. masses when I had snuck shots of wine from the sacristy. It was the only thing that put a smile under my sleepy eyes.

The shuffling of shoes snapped my senses and had awakened me to the gathered gazing at the sky. There had been no official announcement declaring the funeral's conclusion. No one to inform everyone they were invited to the next-of-kin's house to indulge in a mountain of comfort food. No one to rescue the spouse from the echoes of the deceased after the guests had gone home, and only ghosts and footprints remained. Nor was there anyone to explain to a fifth grader what the day and death meant.

On the return to the church, I discovered that no noise was louder than the one inside my head. The discord pierced my dreams: the closing of the casket, the wailing, an unknown journey into eternity, a leap from the bridge, the cacophony of sounds scattered across the scene, Grandpa's funeral, and the many I had served since then.

When we arrived, I ran to rid the smell of flowers, to erase the corpse's face, and to shake the sting of death. I ran to the sanctuary and searched for the wine. I ran with the river and the fruit truck in mind. I ran as fast as my torn tennis shoes allowed. I ran with the hope to rejoin a football game.

I searched for dates which shared my birthday.

CHAPTER 5

When I wasn't running from my mother or running to funerals and obsessing over the mystery of death, I spent time living and dying in sports, music, and movies—alternatives which pulled me away from my home, school, and the neighborhood.

My earliest experiences began in a large greenspace adjacent to a shopping center behind my aunt Evelyn's house. I spent days playing chase and baseball in the high grass before it had been paved into a parking lot.

"You can practice with us," I remember Mr. Bush saying. He volunteered to coach the Indians, a team comprised of cousins and brothers in and around the neighborhood. He let me hang out in right field, where I returned fly balls and grounders which had rolled my way.

"With the older boys?" I asked.

"Yes. I've watched you throw the ball, and you're better than some of the ones I already have."

"What do you want me to do?" I asked. He looked down at me as I looked up, chewing on a leather glove string still stained with lunchtime chili, compliments of another near-death experience. Energized by the thought of being around baseball, I had dashed to the station wagon, glove in one hand, chili dog in the other. Amid the bustle, I failed to check my seat belt. And the door. Out I flew when my mom turned from Americus Street, rolling across onto the Monroe Street's centerline. There I lay dying in disappointment, crying over my hot dog sitting sixty feet away, while holding tightly to the bun.

"Pitch batting practice and just get the ball over the plate," Mr. Bush said. He limped with each prosthetic step, a mannequin-looking leg I had seen in store windows.

I knew little about pitching mechanics, but I knew baseball and football, and throwing the two were in my blood. Year after year, they had taken me lands away from funerals, family feuds, and neighborhood fights. When I crossed the chalked lines, I entered another universe—played out at Mel Ott and McDonoghville Parks. My mother was reportedly related to Mr. Ott, the Gretna Hall of Famer who was the first National Leaguer to surpass five hundred home runs. Each time I entered a batter's box, I pretended something fluid had passed from his bat to mine. Whether it was blood, fate, or wishful thinking, one thing was certain—baseball beckoned at an early age, and I had taken to the game as naturally as a bird takes to flight.

I thought Mr. Bush was joking, letting a younger kid pitch, especially to my older brother, David, who had given me the opportunity to be there. He took me everywhere. We were shadows. Mine was darker, but his extended further. Our early sports days were spent playing together, until life had thrown us in different directions. Pitching to him was a scary ball of emotions. I had been happy in the outfield, chewing on the chili glove, minding my own business.

The ball came off the bat barrel faster than it did for the pitches to reach the plate. In Mel Ott fashion, they sprayed pitches right and left. I wanted to mow 'em down, emulating Bob Gibson, seventeen strikeouts in the World Series opener. The game played out on a TV no larger than a shoebox in Mr. Dugas's garage. I watched as he placed a patch on my bike tire for twenty-five cents but charged me nothing to use the air hose.

"Good job, kid!" Mr. Bush hollered.

"But they're hitting the ball all over the field," I yelled. Tears formed. A fire raged in my stomach. A will to be the best ached with each breath, and at the same time, I had fallen in love with a ball, a bat, and a glove.

Over the years, I was fortunate to have placed trophies on our living room mantel. They stood in the strange company below a Catholic crucifix and above a double-barreled shotgun and a vinyl record player. The awards were reminders of All-Star Teams, victories and defeats, championships and last place finishes, and the will to compete in a hundred-degree heat and humidity while wearing 100 percent cotton uniforms, number "7" stitched in the middle. They served for potential good times to come. And nothing and nobody could take that away.

But trophies collected dust. And my mother despised dust and dirt more than she loved her son's athletic awards.

*****

Music was on every doorstep and in every nook 'n' New Orleans cranny. Like sports, the vibes were going places where I was free to be myself. Beats and themes stayed planted in my head. The tunes became interwoven with my language and humor. By high school and beyond, I morphed into a romantic which described my state of affairs—a culture captivated by infatuation and heartache, war and peace, and good love gone badly. Music taught me how life had been and how it's supposed to be. And I bought it.

My first turn-on was radio tunes. I'd spend the daylight listening to Top 40 hits, and the midnight hour with my ear against the transistor trying to catch Beaker Street. On a clear evening, I could catch the channel airing out of Little Rock. Mysterious "space music" played in the background during disc jockey conversations. This was my baptism into acid music, since "Beaker" was known to be an LSD lab tube. Although my radio tunes were diverse, blues, blues rock, soul, and New Orleans Funk were my mainstays.

But my desire to *listen* to music was eventually exceeded by the inspiration to *play* music. On visits to downtown Gretna when my dad needed to buy parts for our Rambler, I'd stand salivating in front of the Western Auto window, soaking in a simple Pearl drum kit.

Western was a multipurpose store adjacent to a couple of my favorite places—Tower Theater and a record store. In time, the main street store faded, put out of business by a mall, much the same as our baseball practice field. But the sight of the Professional Pearl drums rocked me to sleep, and during warm November and December days, they called my name.

"Come on, Perry," I said.

"Where to?" he asked.

"What you say about WA?" It was music to his ears. His love for the harmonica was harmonious to my love for the skins.

We rode our bikes on the levee, racing barges and freighters fighting an unforgiving current. We passed fuel facilities, which had transported petroleum to boats. My mind flashed to summer days when we assembled a "dirty dozen division," lunch bags in tow:

Krauts hid atop titanic tanks and warehouses—shooting at us from every angle. We battled until the bastards fell to the ground, until victory was ours. Our band of brothers suffered minimal casualties. We covered them in white sheets and slid their bodies off a pier into the dark water below. Perry played taps on his imaginary harp. We wiped our tears on the way to the ferry, while whistling tunes past the German graveyard.

"We need to form a band one day," I said. Perry and I sat on our bikes, lost in a trance of drums and harmonicas in the Western window. "You can play bass and the harp. I'll lay down the backbeat."

"Want it to be a blues band?" he asked.

"Yes, sir. We need to find a cat who can slide and slither up and down the guitar. Deal?"

"Deal." We extended hands. We believed a handshake was as good and as golden as a Gibson guitar.

*****

In a good year and a little luck, my siblings and I received a Christmas gift. Having been taught and reminded that some children in the world have nothing, being grateful was our way of life. My will was tested when cousins boasted and paraded possessions in front of my face. Shame heightened my insecurity, but it also forced me to take refuge in something as simple as a drum skins—a basic kit, filled with dreams of setting my soul free.

"You like them?" David asked.

"Like? I love 'em," I said. Save for the stereo, it was the only semblance of a musical instrument to have entered our house. A thousand times I had lain my ear pressed to the speakers. Once I established a song's rhythm, I'd imitate the beat on my air drums.

"Go put them in your room and make sure the damn door is shut when you play," my mom said. My feet never touched the floor; pent-up desire released from me. Within minutes, I started playing, then came to the realization that the toy skins were a far cry from a plush kit. Within days, I realized playing drums was nothing more than a pipe dream. "That's enough! I'm tired of the racket! That's too much goddamn noise!" my mom screamed. My playing must have been worse than I thought.

"But you said I could play! Why did you buy them, if I can't play them?"

"I'll have Bill or Bobby throw them away or place them on the street," she said. I did what I did best. I ran to the river.

I sat against a bridge column upholding the abutment three hundred feet above. Each vehicle's fate rested on its base and shoulders, and the rumble of wheels kept pace with my heart. Water filled my eyes. The blue firmament reflected diamonds from the river.

Just keep telling yourself, she can take the drums out of the house, but she can't take the drums out of me. She can take the drums out of the house, but she can't take the drums out of me. She can...she can't...

*****

Being an actor had become my ultimate picture of dreams, especially since the drums had been reduced to a symbolic cymbal. By the time Bob Ewell had spit in Atticus Finch's face, I made an oath I would one day be in the movies. Scout, Jem, and Dill showed me that children had a chance to be in films. A cousin taught me about them during bedtime readings of *To Kill a Mockingbird*. When I heard the movie was playing at the Tower, I begged to go see it.

I plopped two quarters on the ticket counter to a lady who wore glasses, chewed gum, and popped bubbles. I waved good-bye and skipped to a painted Celtic spiral, imitating the Tin Man in search of a heart, rigid and helpless. I pretended to be the Lion seeking courage on my return trip. My family yelled for me to hurry inside, or I'd miss the cartoon, which preceded the movie.

Each time I visited the Tower, I indulged in a Dr. Pepper and popcorn. With precision, I'd dip a kernel into the crushed ice. The treat lasted until Boo Radley saved Scout, or a cowboy rode in to save the day. I sat cross-legged, which allowed me a clear view of movies the same color as the audience—black and white.

"Hey, E. White!' I hollered. The theater lights had come on after Boo and Scout held hands while sitting on a southern porch swing. E. White looked away while his arms hung over the balcony. The scene was a carbon copy from the movie, save for Jem, Scout, and Dill. I had drawn stares, and a backhand stung the side of my crew cut. My eyes stayed affixed on my friend.

E. White had the personality of a lakefront summer breeze, soft and sweet. His teeth were a striking contrast to his skin, and he had the longest arms at St. Anthony. He and his sister were in my classes since we had started in 1961. She had difficulty holding her bladder and a tougher time telling the teacher she needed to use the restroom. Kids pointed fingers when she sat in a wet circle, which dripped to the floor, as tears dripped from her eyes. I was taught that they lived on "the other side" of the railroad tracks, which confused me, because so did we.

"Hey, E. White! Why do you have to drink from that fountain?" I asked. Monday morning's recess had arrived. Saturday's *Mockingbird* movie remained on my playlist.

"I don't know," he said. He looked at a sign that directed him to his fountain, but it never explained why. I saw the pain in his eyes. His face taught me a lesson in civility.

"I saw you at the movie Saturday. When I grow up, I'm gonna be an actor."

"Me, too," he said.

"Can you picture us as cowboys?"

"Yeah!"

"Hey, E. White! Let's ride!"

"Right on!"

We jumped on our legendary horses. I chose black. He chose white. Both had black saddles and black, leather bridles. We blazed a trail along our theater screen, kicking dust and bad guy's butts, until our stallions had grown tired and thirsty.

"What ya say we tie 'em up and give 'em some water, Partner Pete?" I asked. "We can use your fountain. Water's probably fresher."

"Sho thang, Tex!" E. White said.

Later that night, I placed my hands behind my head, exhausted from a long day of acting. I wondered who had my pillow, as I watched cockroaches hang from the ceiling. A brother's knee poked me in the back.

I closed my eyes and pictured E. White and me making movies. I pictured us robbing the rich and giving to the poor. I pictured us luckier than the Lucky Strikes we smoked sitting upon our saddles. I pictured our pictures on posters, movie lights shining on our sequin suits and six-shooters.

But mostly, I pictured us at high noon—E. White on his screen and me on mine, in theaters miles apart, like water fountains at our Catholic school.

*****

Movies showed me. Music told me. Sports allowed me. All three taught me. And each had awakened me to an emotion I was instructed to disavow—attractive ladies were an aphrodisiac. This was poisonous for a boy who wore his emotions on his sleeve, forever creating the conflict of "how something so good was taught to be so bad."

With her square jaw and cheekbones, lashes and dark eyes, Katherine Hepburn's face was a moonbeam, which radiated across the silver screen. She was the first female in film who captured and kept my attention. My popcorn and my mind were sent packing to a planet I craved to visit. And while I had taken her to my dreams, Ms. Hepburn reminded me I didn't have to leave planet earth. I had already been told and learned firsthand.

"Would you like to carry my books?" Sue asked. She descended from a school bus one day and called me aside. "It's only a little way, 'bout a block. These things are too heavy for me to get up the steps."

"Sure." I wondered if all high schools had girls as beautiful, and how I couldn't wait to get there if they did.

"You're so adorable," Sue said. I underestimated the weight of the books, but the attention provided a morsel of confidence since the drums had been discarded. New skin now replaced the drum skins, arousing a sensation I naturally acknowledged. "Are you seven?"

"Just turned nine. And I'm strong, too." I displayed my mountainous bicep—the size of a green pea. I strutted my stuff, a rooster who ruled the roost, and hoped the neighborhood boys were watching from the corner store. I watched her blonde hair sway hip to hip, skimming the pockets of her faded blue jeans.

"Pretty big muscle, kid. Bet all the girls fight over you, but I'll keep them away," Sue said. The steps to her second-floor, double shotgun house were more mountainous than my bicep. She climbed, leaving me gasping for breath I thought would never come.

"I'll take them now," she said. She grabbed the books, planted one leg against the front door, and propped the screen door with the other. Sue slammed both.

Undefeated. That was my attitude. I considered my uncle Willie's philosophy: "If a girl hurts you, get off the bus and stay off. They'll be another one waiting at the next stop." After Sue shut the door, his words provided the courage for me to ride to Debbie's house and knock on their screened door, which had hung on a single hinge.

Debbie was the finest girl in a five-block radius, perhaps five miles. She placed Ms. Hepburn and others on hold. The closest rival was her sister, Kathy, whose mean streak Debbie daily incurred. "Cat" ruled a house the size of ours but with fewer children and a mom who out-hollered mine. But none of that mattered. I had Deb dibs as the unbeaten quarterback who sported football pants, while his helmet and shoulder pads kept his bike company.

For two hours before heading to the ballpark, we practiced kissing while sitting on the sofa and listening to the radio. Since we had decided that repetition would bring near perfection, we occasionally surfaced for air and discussed technique. If a change of scenery was invited, we climbed a tree house that overlooked the railroad cars, and where the sun set behind the riverbend, where the freighters floated, and we made plans to take a slow boat to China. Life seemed freer up there than it did on the ground.

Following our lip-stretching sessions, Deb and I pushed my bike to Monday practices. She never made a game. She never had a ride. She was my number one fan who stood at the fence watching me hand the ball to J. R., the tailback who outran all our competition. He had the speed of a greyhound and was a male version of Sue—blonde hair and a killer smile. And he was the reason we were undefeated with one game remaining to capture an undefeated season and a championship.

"Well, we won it all. Ten wins and no losses," I said. One week removed from our final game, Deb and I sat on her front steps. Clouds covered the sun, and a detached mood covered her face. "Wish you could have been there. Toss right to J. R. Toss left to J. R. Touchdown!" Signs of life shown when I detailed our tailback's exploits.

"I want to go steady," she said. My eyes grew larger than a blitzing linebacker.

Me? Steady with Debbie? Pay dirt! Quarterback gets the girl! My heart danced in the end zone.

"Yes! So, would—"

"I'd like to go steady," she interrupted. "But not with you. I want to go steady with J. R."

Wind flushed my tears on the bike ride home. The sting of "not being good enough" slapped my face. I passed bus stop after bus stop, not one girl waited. Two weeks later, J. R. won the MVP. Debbie sat next to him at the banquet; don't know how she got there. The following year, we lost every game.

CHAPTER 6

Before supermarkets and grocery chains competed for an expanding market and girls played me like a Stradivarius, corner stores were a New Orleans staple—a cultural pillar embedded in a neighborhood's soul. Corner stores were time-savers, a closer walk to purchase food, smokes, meds, milk, and more. They also served as a social gathering where adolescents and kids met to make important decisions.

"What game are we playing today?" Greg asked. "Not-It-on-Bikes" was my favorite, until my ankle landed in the spokes, tossing me onto a sidewalk. I was forced to ride the bench during a five-thirty ballgame I had been scheduled to pitch. The coach kept giving me the "how could you be so stupid" look. I sat in guilt watching my team get smoked by the ten-run rule.

"Hide the Belt," David said first.

Why do we have to play that, when we get so many whippings at home? I thought. Homerun Derby, Rock War at the cannery, and Knuckles were a few that came to mind, but I dare not say anything, knowing they wouldn't listen. Most of them would have chastised me for opening my mouth. I was caught in a trap of wanting to fit in while surrendering to them "letting me be there," as long as I understood who pissed the furthest. Between home and their company, I was developing a complex. But the games raised my confidence. It was the one place where I pissed further than them. It was the one place where they knew I fit in. Perhaps, they were envious of a kid who not only matched them but often surpassed them athletically.

We played the games since I had been in second grade. They were an extension of sports, which taught me to play by the rules, how to compete, and how to adapt in the moment. But when the fun was finished, I never realized I could have walked away from the shaming and teasing and needing their approval. I was blinded by the fact that everything counted and not yet wise enough to understand that none of it mattered. But it was better than being alone.

A moment of silence hovered, as if by remote control we could all see the wheels spinning in our heads. We sat on Ms. Helen's corner store steps, White boys sandwiched between two Black neighborhoods. We were her frequent customers. In return, she let us gather to eat our fully dressed po'boy sandwiches—drenched in mayo and mustard. Barq's Root Beer or Crème Soda eased the foot longs down our throats. Adding pleasure to gluttony, we devoured a fresh Hubig's pie. Save for my mama's gumbo, I rarely tasted a better moment. The silence was broken when Gary walked toward us with a grave look on his face.

"Some guy sucker punched Bubbie with a beer bottle last night in the Dairy Queen parking lot," Gary said. Dairy Queen was the king of vanilla shakes, Friday night fast cars and turf wars. "He lost two front teeth and a buncha blood. Man, his lips and nose are fucked up. He's in West Jeff Hospital."

The good and the bad of the neighborhood also kept me in a state of imbalance—fleeting feelings of fun and comfort, punishment and pain. Girls who smiled in my face then broke my heart in the next breath; boys who embraced like brothers then fought at the drop of a hat. No sooner I had felt warm sunshine only to look over my shoulder to feel the lightening and hear the thunder.

"Mel's gonna kill that guy when he finds him," T. Shep said.

Bubbie, like my other fatherless neighbors, lived with Mel and their mother. He was bigger than Mel and louder and a loquacious shit-stirrer. I pictured him with glass shards in his mouth, for once unable to speak. Mel was outgoing, and we shared a common trait—a propensity to fight with a nice to nasty disposition. We could both flip the switch at the speed of light.

"Hide the belt it is," Greg declared. We walked to play the game when another face turned the corner.

The last time I had seen Ronnie L., we were playing Homerun Derby in a field beneath the bridge, vehicles echoing above, boats in the distance. Clouds hung ominously over the day; Robert Kennedy's assassination hung heavily on my heart. Later that night, I dreamt every corpse I viewed at funeral homes had risen and invited me to join them.

"Pretty cool, huh?" Ronnie L. asked. The new, black GTO crawled to a stop. Leather seats. Automatic transmission. Eight-track stereo. Chrome wheels—a rocket ready to blast into the future. And I had never seen anything like it, either: the two limbs resting on the edge of the driver's seat. A rod ran from his hands to the brakes and to the accelerator. My anxiety shot up. My mind shut down. Ronnie L., legless at nineteen, and me, six years too young to be drafted.

"Say, bra. Where'd you get this hot rod?" Gary asked.

"Stepped on a mine in 'Nam. Uncle Sam gave it to me and lifetime disability. In three months, I'll move into a house. Freedom ain't free. Hell, not even free from the draft, but I got something out of it," he said.

I thought better than to ask if he'd rather have his legs, but at least he didn't have to endure Hide the Belt. Ronnie L. cranked the engine and Hendrix beyond comprehension, punched the gas, and laid rubber down Americus Street. All that power and limited freedom to use it.

The sudden joy and sorrow of seeing Ronnie L. dissipated after the game. Welts appeared on my legs from the belt blows. I searched for reasons why things happened the way they did. A month later, Gary and Greg enlisted, perhaps to avoid Vietnam, perhaps to keep their lives and limbs. I was left to fight the battles in my own labyrinth, including the ones at church and school. On most days, I reminded myself that it was better than fighting in a jungle a thousand miles away.

*****

Every Friday morning, we marched to nine thirty mass, Catholic soldiers wearing St. Anthony uniforms—boys in khakis and white T-shirts, the school name printed across the chest. Girls wore brown skirts, white blouses and socks. The school and the church were the centerpieces of the parish, but I never looked forward to attending the mandatory masses. Most Sundays, I went screaming, while my mother and religion kicked every step of the way. The strict rules and incantations left a hole in my soul, which, in time, the God-man Jesus filled. Grades K-12 cured me of Catholicism. Spiritually, I checked out before high school graduation.

But there I was, following class by class into the historic structure, which had gone twelve rounds with heavyweight Hurricane Betsy, leaving a gaping hole in the roof and displacing much of its lumber. Student by student, we would genuflect before taking a seat on the pew.

"Our Father who art in heaven," a voice screamed. It rose above the incense and candle smoke.

"Who's praying so loudly?" I asked Jay.

"Sounds like Harry," he said. Jay was my closest school friend who packed a powerful punch and lived in Gretna Park, a suburban section of town. On an occasional Friday, I'd ride the school bus for an overnight stay. I felt uncertain how to act in a place different from mine—hardwood floors, real drums in his carpeted bedroom, and parents who never fought.

"Forgive us our trespasses as we forgive those who trespass against us!" Harry continued. He stood center church, shaved head, squared jaw, an angelic silhouette made certain by the sunlight which had penetrated the stained glass windows.

"It's not time for that prayer," I said.

"Wonder what's wrong," Jay said.

"Dang, devil's got him," I said.

"Turn around boys and girls. Harry's having a spell," Mrs. BF demurred. Her blue, greyish hair reached the bottom of Harry's chest. He was the tallest boy in the school as a third grader. People unkindly taunted him as a brainless oaf.

"Maybe he's having one of Ms. BF's spelling B's," I joked. Jay suppressed his laughter. Spelling B competition had thrived under my skin due to my inability to spell "rhythm." Regardless of my second-place finishes, Miss BF always consoled me, calling me "cutie pie" and smart. She and other teachers chose me over other students to help with extra duties.

None showed more attention than Ms. Le Faso, my sixth-grade teacher who had an hourglass figure, a face designed for the movies, and a smile that could light up a screen. She had taken me and Ricky Do to a night parade, three of us side by side in her '55 Chevy. He sat next to her on the way. On the return, we clutched beads and laughed about my becoming a flambeaux carrier—masters of sparks with torches spraying particles into the crowd. Me, King Flamboyant, getting to dance with fire, not a penny in my pocket. But the fire felt hottest sitting hip to hip with my teacher. Her face reflected from the bridge lights. I wondered why she invited two Richards when she had others to ask.

Nuns descended on Harry. They stepped on toes while bulldozing their way toward him. One shook him hard enough to make me dizzy. Sister Lucina, whom I dubbed Attila the Nun, was the most feared. She was a Kodiak size lady and had a bad habit of being "hands on" and was notorious for throwing her weight around.

"Did I not tell you to shut up?" she asked Harry. She escorted him to the rear; her rosary beads followed behind swinging left to right. A thud echoed the way Mel Ott's bat met a fastball. They walked toward us on the return. "Get here in the communion line! And I better not hear another word, or it will be worse next time," she said. Harry stood between Jay and me. I did my best to look away from the bruise above his ear.

Sister Lucina's shadow suffocated the sunlight. Our eyes met. We were boxers standing at center ring; our pupils were filled with hate. Her jaws pulsated with each heavy breath. If looks could kill, one of us would have died. Maybe Attila had not been informed of the many beatings I endured. She surely was unaware that I had sworn to never take another without recompense.

Be still. If she grabs you, go low. Get under her tunic. Work the ribs. Keep punching, until she cries for mercy. The way Harry couldn't. In the background, the priest distributed the heavenly host—"The Body of Christ" intonated in a Latin language.

*****

Years prior to her banging Harry's head against the church wall, Sister Lucina carried a crying and screaming Stephen H. to the only empty seat in kindergarten—the one next to me. "Let's sit you here next to this nice boy," she said. Stephen settled down in days ahead, but some kids cried and suffered from the bullying and teasing during their time at St. Anthony Grammar School.

"Punch him in the balls, chickenshit," Bully BJ demanded. He was a sixteen-year-old sixth grader from Hope Haven, a foster home adjacent to a high school in Marrero. His tight pants and tighter T-shirt accentuated his muscular frame and exposed his hairy armpits. His commands were never ignored by the bunch who hid in his shadow.

Ambushes were discreet, occurring at the corners of the playground, or when a teacher exited her room. H. R. stood at the rear of his class, circled by a school of sharks. He was their magnet, and they loathed him—his drooped shoulders, limped wrist, curly hair, thick waistline, girlish gait, braces, and a voice to match each feature.

"Quit whining, big baby!" BJ said. He landed his fist on H. R.'s crotch. The more H. R. shrilled, the more they pummeled. The vertex of his screams shattered when he sat on a trap of thumbtacks they had hidden on his desk.

Similar attacks hailed from behind a tree during recess when they punched him, pinched him, pulled his hair, and kicked him. Just for the hell of it. Walton would have been proud. I wasn't. I was perhaps the worst of them, doing nothing except being a bystander indifferently watching him get stoned.

H. R. was not alone. On many days, the chant "Rock! Rock! Rock!" rained on the opposite end of the playground. My black sheep brother, Bobby, encountered his share of abuse. His peers and their followers formed a circle too big and strong for me to penetrate. They pushed and shoved him from punk to punk.

I had learned that cowards came in all shapes and sizes—those who led and those who followed, apart from each other, they could do nothing. And there were those like me, a kid witnessing hatred, a kid who could fight but chose not to.

*****

St. Anthony's Spring Fair was a Men's Club fundraiser on steroids. More importantly, it was the club's kindred spirit with free faucets and opened doors. By the time I had reached eighth grade, I searched for ways and things to pacify the pain and calm the confusion in my life—for medicine or someone to replace the guilt and lack of love I was experiencing. The fair was a potential pathway to peace.

Darkness descended upon the booths and games, and the dim fair lights dulled the eyes. Beer slowed the senses and accelerated the laughter among the older folk. High school awaited three months away; it was my last elementary school chance, time for me to make my move or be SOL.

"There's Herzog, our quarterback!" Coach Mike yelled. He wore slacks, dress shoes, and a beer belly.

"Some could pass. Some could throw. He did both," Coach Nick said. He wore a bigger beer belly and a mustache, which swallowed his face.

They coached my undefeated Green team, and they were far better than Mr. Ed who coached the Red team two years prior. During punishment lap twenty-one, I decided I'd no longer take his "son-of-a-bitching" us each time the offensive line got the snap count incorrect. My parents religiously "son-of-a-bitched," but they never called us one. I walked away with his voice echoing "son of a bitch." The Green team coaches reignited my desire to play.

"He was like Archie Manning on offense and Dick Butkus on defense. Passive aggressive! Pun intended!" Coach Mike said. They looked lit and looped.

"Get us a beer, will ya, kid?" Coach Nick asked. *Bingo! How did they ask me, an eighth grader?* The sun had disappeared behind the New Orleans skyline. I walked to concessions and passed the city's beer requirement test—tall enough to see over the counter.

"What are you doing with three beers?" Coach Mike asked.

"Got one for my dad," I said. I moved to the opposite side of the school and became acquainted with a dark corner and downed the liquid upright.

One became two, and two had become one too many. Heat lightning struck across the orange, curtained sky as I exited the school gate. I relied on familiar steps to guide me home—steps I had walked during school lunchtime, a cup of soup, and a sandwich waiting on the table.

But that night's excursion was no picnic. I danced down the middle of my moonlit "neutral ground," a New Orleans, grassed-covered median. I stumbled upon a cigarette butt, which brought back a lesson learned—my mom making me and David smoke "the entire goddamn pack" of non-filtered Camels. We had been enjoying our newly learned vice taught by our older neighbors, until my younger brother ratted us out. My mom locked the living room door and left us to smoke and choke. After the second cig, David looked green, and I prayed for death, to send me up with the vapor which engulfed me.

One dead vice led to another. In my first state of drunkenness, the worst in life surfaced. Four blocks from the fair, the journey home reopened wounds and memories. Beer's good medicine provided a mighty high and the blues to supplement it. The closer I came to our front porch, the more I hoped high school would present a do-over.

"What's the matter with you?" my mother asked.

"Madder? I'm not mad," I stammered.

"I said, 'M-A-T-T-E-R?'" she spelled.

"I could use you at my spelling B," I said. I had fallen face first onto the bedcover.

"Have you been drinking?" she asked.

"Are you kidding? How can I get beer?"

"Who said anything about beer?"

"Shit! Why are you always asking me questions?" I asked.

"Now you're cussing? I better not hear you cuss again!"

"Well, hell. You taught me. Go get your damn belt, Barbara Pearl Harbor Herzog! That's what you do best, always bombing my ass!"

Had she used a bullwhip, I was too numb to feel the sting, too dizzy to stop the room from spinning. My temple throbbed, and my head felt larger than my body. My breath swam in a cesspool; the beer remnants remained stuck in my throat. I bypassed the *Our Father* and the *Hail Mary*. I went straight to Jesus and begged him to take me in the middle of the night.

The next morning, my athletic trophies were gone.

Part 2

CHAPTER 7

"Hey, Herzog. Put this condom box on her desk, man," a fellow classmate said. It was my freshman year, 1971, when again, another element of surprise placed me in a moment of shock and confusion.

"A what?" I asked.

"This condom box, bra."

It was my first time to have seen one, live and in color, though I had heard about condoms in the neighborhood. Only weeks into high school when yesterday's street talk had become that day's real-ity—condoms—an abrupt introduction to the antithesis of Catholic contraception.

It was my first time to have held one. An inscription "Go Down in Flames" rested against the setting sun. Pelicans flew above a coast-line. It had an alluring power. In seconds, I thought how I could impress my classmates and win a host of new friends.

"Go ahead, bra. Everyone will laugh their asses off," he said. His voice had an ominous yet convincing tone. "Hurry. She's about to enter the room." Two other voices inside my head waged war and added to the confusion; one whispered, while one screamed. The church taught me they were the Holy Spirit and Satan. I called them Mr. Right and Mr. Wrong.

A chill shuddered throughout my body, as my teacher entered the classroom. She moved at the speed of a bayou, a slow stream car-peted across the Gulf Coast region. A tight skirt was painted around her hips. Her breasts shifted neither an inch north or south within her blouse, which could not be said of her backside when she wrote notes upon the chalkboard. Throughout the day, she had told me months later, she edited her work, so my class could have a perfect lesson.

"Please open your books to page," she started. Then stopped. Her face paled. I sat up and took a deep breath.

"What page?" A bucktoothed boy wearing thick glasses had raised his hand. A rescue wish cried from her countenance. Nobody came forward. She had the same look victims have when the dust settles after delinquents had left their marks.

"Gentleman, I need you to stay in your seat. Get up only if it's urgent. Use the restroom only if it's an emergency. Do you understand?"

"Yes, ma'am," the bucktoothed boy and H. R. said.

I exhaled and gave thanks to Mr. Right or the Holy Spirit or both for my having not placed the box there. She made way to the office. Her shoes left an echo across the stillness of the room.

*****

My mother was hell-bent on me and my siblings to get a Catholic education. She was going to do whatever it took for me to attend Archbishop Shaw and stay out of West Jefferson, the public school. Shaw was operated by the Roman Catholic archdiocese of New Orleans. It opened in 1962 and was governed by the Salesians of St. John Bosco, an Italian priest who founded the Preventive System, which was based upon love rather than retribution. All of this and more were music to my mother's ears.

Although my St. Anthony classmates were going to Shaw, and the neighborhood boys attended West Jeff, I held a disdain for both schools, because neither was coed. My choice was decided by my mother, who was not only ecstatic about the religious connotations, but also because the student population was entirely male. But when I entered seventh period English on the first day of school, my attitude changed. It was the first time I had seen Naomi McCarthy Wagenbach, and my world and anything within took on a different meaning.

Room 111 faced southeast and had transparent sliding doors, each adorned with caution tape at its center. Forty yards from my desk sat an outdoor pool, which appeared to have stretched to infinity. Forty yards beyond the pool was the football field. The rippling waves and the smell of grass presented a diversion from my math class, the only other class I had along wing 100. The scenery was a pleasant diversion from anything taught in the school.

Except in her room. Naomi was the daily diversion in a crowded pool of boys in which I swam. I spent most of my time underwater in the deep end, soaking in her illuminated eyes rivaled only by her laugh and spirit. Her smile was a continuous summer, and I was a boy of that season—entranced by heat and storms and swimming and the smack of a ball hitting a glove.

Few ladies compared, save for the *Playboy*s hidden under the soiled mattresses in our Americus Street shed, where David, Perry, and I shared the secret space; we were monks in monasteries with a singular motivation. In their honor, we named our private palace *The Man-ass-stery*. A growing child could go astray in such a hole, isolated in a dream of getting lucky, while studying photos we couldn't find in cheaper, romance magazines.

Mrs. Wagenbach brought the *Playboy* images to life. The same way she did with the lessons she presented. I sat on the sideline while other students peppered her about the injustice given to characters in short stories and novels. Debates would ensue—grace, guilt, legalism, sin, and shame. Back and forth, it would go with accusations and opinions. The volleying often made the Mrs. delightfully dizzy, but she remained consistent in her response:

"People make serious transgressions, like Hester Prynne did in *The Scarlett Letter*, who committed adultery. She deserved harsh punishment and could have run but didn't. Those were the consequences of her choices. Such could be the same for us should we cross that bridge." I decided to enter the fray, when a voice from above interjected.

"Teachers. Students. Please pardon the interruption. This is Mr. B, school disciplinarian. I need Mrs. Wagenbach's sixth and seventh period classes to report to the auditorium. Once again. I need Mrs.

Wagenbach's sixth and seventh period classes to report immediately to the auditorium."

I was curious why two classes were called, while other students murmured that it certainly had something to do with the condom box. On the longest walk of my fourteen years, I whispered thanks to the voice, which stopped me from placing it on her desk and thought how sex education had been the forbidden fruit in school and at home. Catholic knowledge was more seminal than carnal knowledge.

Most of what little I knew concerning sex came from the neighborhood and *Playboy* pictures. Stories and photos, but no real education. I was embarrassed when listening to Perry who had no dad, but he talked about sex like he knew everything. I was ashamed that I had a dad and three older brothers, yet I knew little. What I needed was clarity.

I had determined it would have to be a matter of self-pursuit and discovery, or someone would teach me. This I was to receive from a voice independent from the one that stopped me from placing the condom box on Mrs. Wagenbach's desk.

*****

"All the way to the front, gentlemen. All the way to the front," he said. Mr. B stood holding the door and a poker face—a stare dressed in black glasses and black hair, both which seemed to have been molded by an injection machine.

We resembled a marching band filing into the dark and cold auditorium, until we became Pontchartrain Beach Bumping Cars colliding at the front of the stage. Mr. B howled and flailed his arms while blowing his whistle, shouting new directions. I could not determine who was dumber—freshman following literal instructions or an adult who forgot to instruct us to find a seat.

"Sit up! Place both hands on your knees," he said. The curtain was closed and gave the stage a small face, and the lights had shown over the first two row of seats. My mind traveled to James Cagney being interrogated at a police precinct. "To salvage your instruction time, gentlemen, I'll get to the point. We are uncertain who placed the condom box on Mrs. Wagenbach's desk, but we are certain we will find out. We are giving the student, or students, three days to confess. Failure to do so will result in both classes being expelled."

Mr. B had flipped the switch, catapulting the meek past purgatory, a populous holding pen located between heaven and hell, and directly to eternal damnation. Heads had turned as though everyone arrived at a four-way stop sign without receiving their Last Rites. Tears of fear flowed for those potentially witnessing their Shaw diploma vanishing. I had been to less somber funerals.

An arm raised during Mr. B's heavy-handed condemnation. The disciplinarian returned to his stare, perhaps smelling capitulation, until the hand lowered. "Now I know what you are all thinking, why should all of you suffer for the sins of one or two," Mr. B said. I was thinking how this student, who had raised his hand, must have instantly grown brass balls.

Up shot the hand, again.

"It better be good, guy!" Mr. B screamed. His gaze went through H. R. and dotted every eye in a seat.

Six-foot-three-inch H. R. stumbled toward the isle, crushing toes along the way. Mr. B stuck his chest out in a mission accomplished fashion. Until H. R. tripped and fell to his chubby cheeks.

"Return to your seat and sit down!" he yelled.

"I have to go to the restroom! Mrs. Wagenbach said we could go anytime, if it's an emergency!" the boy squealed.

H. R. did nothing to conceal the brown spot on the rear of his khakis. Nor could we conceal our laughter, even as Mr. Disciplinarian raised both hands in the auditorium air.

*****

The crap had also hit the fan. An administrator had issued an extreme ultimatum, a near-death sentence for some. I was living my Adam and Eve thoughts, angry with an injustice that so many had to suffer because of one or two people—to the point where I was ready to fall on a sword and admit it was me—until I remembered the teacher who had been harmed by it all.

Perhaps the worst part was that my mother had yet to hear the news. Nor was I ready to explain the consequences should nobody confess. But by the time I arrived home, I still had no idea if Mr. B and company had done due diligence to have captured the condom culprit. And I had no idea how they would inform parents. So, I sucked it up and made sure she heard it from me and with my fingers crossed, hidden behind my back.

"A what?" she asked.

"A condom box," I replied.

"Jesus, Joseph, and Mary!" Her jaw dropped, and her shoulders sagged. My mom had a way of aging when confronted with adversity. "You had anything to do with this?" I expected the question, given my extensive criminal record; all of which she was quick to recount.

"No, ma'am. I don't even know what a condom box is," I said. "But it must be serious, because we're all getting expelled if nobody's caught or admits it." I skipped the part where I *almost* placed it on the teacher's desk. Much the same way I had hid that church wine, and not beer, had been my very first taste of alcohol during my altar boy days. Experience had become a decent lesson by then.

"You better be telling the truth, because if you had anything to do with it, you will be spending the next four years at West Jefferson. Jesus! Your first semester in high school and you might get expelled? Son of a bitch!"

"There's no way I'm going to *that* school. All my St. Anthony classmates are at Shaw! All Greg and Gary talked about when they were there were the race riots. What about the moral guidance I'll miss? And weekly communion? And what about baseball and football?" Tears dripped from my chin, all the way to my bed, where I hid my face from the world.

But all that water flow had nothing to do with my mother or West Jeff or Shaw or St. Anthony. I could not have cared less about those meaningless matters. I simply had to *act* like I cared. I could have captured my first Academy Award with the performance, knowing what only mattered was the possibility of losing my English teacher. After all, no teacher anywhere looked so good, and no teacher hurt so badly because of a condom box.

CHAPTER 8

Mrs. Wagenbach sat with her legs folded. A pen rested on her lips, and papers were propped on her lap. Fatigue held to her face. I stood outside her room entrance watching her struggle to stay awake, while shoveling gravel with my platform shoes.

"Hello," she said. Her voice had floated across the evening air. Although I rehearsed my lines throughout the day, I became a stage fright actor who lacked the Academy Award confidence I had performed with my mother. I had cold feet on a warm afternoon, and it was too late to have turned back, especially since I had purposely missed the school bus. "Richard?"

"Ah. Hi. Ah, Mrs. Wagenbach. I was wondering…wondering," I stammered.

"It's okay. Come in. Come closer. I'm trying to grade papers." Her classroom was sparsely decorated—a petite Globe Theater replica, an American flag front and center. Being raised in my Madison and American Street houses, I cared nothing about room décor; the walls could have resembled an LSD trip, and I would have been equally as apathetic. I approached and saw that her skirt had lifted. She did nothing to alter her position. Nor did I.

"I've been wanting to apologize," I said. "I walked toward your desk with the box, but something told me to stop. I should have thrown it in the garbage, but I returned it to the person who gave it to me. So, I'm sorry for not throwing it away."

"No need to apologize for something you didn't do, but I would like to know who gave it to you." A long pause ensued, interrupted by the sound of football whistles—reminding me that our freshman season had ended, reminding me of how little playing time I had logged—leaving me to consider if I'd ever again play a game I loved.

"I only came to see how you were doing and to make sure you were okay. Sorry I bothered you. I'll let you be." Missing the bus and having to walk back to McDonoghville seemed shortsighted now, as Mrs. Wagenbach walked toward me.

"Wait. Please wait!" she said. "Try to forget that I asked. I'm somewhat better. Thank you. Believe it or not, you've been the only person to check on me. Not even the administration has checked."

The New Orleans evening sun had shifted further west, breathing rays between the gymnasium and her room. A slant of light slipped between the doorframes and landed softly on her cheek, further amplifying her angelic face. For a split second, I saw Ms. La Faso waving to floats, begging masked men to throw trivial treasure. Mrs. Wagenbach held a pensive pose, holding together hope in which she could rescue me, too—from the beatings, funerals, fighting parents, a man who jumped, rejections, repetitive religion, a dog mauling, and the near death of falling from a car.

Perhaps the worst were the beatings, since they had come from the two who had brought me into the world. For years, I experienced love and acceptance issues, where I felt that no matter what I had done for someone, it was never enough. Standing at the door was a step toward moving past the low self-esteem—believing she would accept me for who I was and what I wore and where I lived and that I had something to offer in spite of it all.

During that 1971 moment, I was uncertain where fantasy and reality converged and where one canceled the other. But I was certain I ached because she ached, and I wanted to make it better for both of us. I was uncertain where childhood ended and adolescence began, but in my young mind, I was certain she was the bridge between the two. I was uncertain how I'd get home, but I was certain I would have crawled the fourteen miles fourteen times, as I saw her standing there, leaning against the door. In a foolish yet absolute way, I felt I could *will it* into existence.

"How are you getting home?" she asked.

"Don't know. If I could call my mother, she'd tell me to take the city bus. I don't have any money to do either."

"Where do you live?"

"Old Gretna. Three blocks from the bridge," I said.

"Oh. I cross the bridge every day. I can take you home."

"I hate to be a bother. I can hitchhike."

"That would be dangerous. Don't be silly. I'll take you there."

"Only if you let me carry your schoolwork. I have experience with that," I said.

She nodded. Grading papers would have to wait.

The day's clamor had settled into clouds of calm. We walked toward the parking lot with deliberate steps and stilled voices. The silence awakened my insecurities in the company of the opposite gender. The lack of conversation made my mind race faster than my heart, which flopped at the speed of a hummingbird's wings.

Her 1972 burnt orange Mercury sat alone on the first row of the rear parking lot. The two-door, chromed wheels and vinyl top looked dealership delivered. The sight of her machine was the only thing I heard since we had left her classroom.

The smell of a new car was foreign to me, and I got a good taste of it when I placed her schoolwork on the rear seat. My car life had been limited to the family station wagons with rusted floorboards, stained seats, and roll-your-own windows. When fully occupied, the wagon was crowded with more humanity than the law allowed. Seniority dictated seating. I landed in the tailgate and faced the rear—nothing to see but what had already been seen in front of me—the way it sometimes looked during limo and streetcar riding. The scanty tailgate space became my imaginary playground to and from New Orleans Saint's games:

Fourth and goal to go from the seven. No timeouts. Two seconds left on the clock. Down by four; Saints need a touchdown to win. Herzog places his hands under the center and barks the signals. Ball's snapped. He rolls right. Parker open in the back of the end zone! Herzog fires!

Touchdown! Touchdown! Saints win! Saints win! Tulane Stadium is in fandemonium!

Mrs. Wagenbach opened her door and sighed when she hit the seat. She tossed her purse and slid her legs under the steering wheel. Her skirt ran up. Again. "Do you like it?" she asked.

"Yes. I've never seen anything like it." My mind had gone to decadent, backseat thinking, as though I had jumped from my teenage years to adulthood, sitting nervously next to a fully grown, physically mature woman. I felt powerless.

"Yep. I like this car, too." She placed the car in gear and drove toward black and blue skies which rained sheets and strands of electricity.

"Have you heard this new song?" she asked. "It's 'Alone Again Naturally.'"

"Who sings it?" I asked.

"I think it's Gilbert O'Sullivan."

I shook my head, straining to hear the lyrics and the melody, both distorted within the Harvey Canal Tunnel, a passageway from Marrero to Gretna. Titanic water drops splattered the windshield when we crossed the centerline. I visualized a tugboat above, struggling, pushing barges through the narrow channel locks. "He has a unique voice," I said.

"I love it," she said, hands on the wheel, head and shoulders bopping and bouncing, impervious to the storm. Two years later, I came to understand why she loved the song, as my life unfolded, playing its lead character snared in a pattern of isolation and excruciating desolation. Shattered into a plethora of pieces, trapped in an inescapable time passage.

"Do you know that I'm much better at keeping rhythm than spelling rhythm?" I asked.

"Why is that?" She seemed rejuvenated, perhaps because somebody had shown some concern, and that somebody was me.

"Born that way. I can cut a rug, too. I've never told anyone, but I believe I'm one-third Black female." She laughed and complimented my Louis Armstrong voice.

"What I meant was, why do you have a hard time spelling it?" she asked.

"Oh, I can spell *it*. I just can't spell *rhythm*." Mrs. Wagenbach giggled at my word play, and I laughed along knowing I was making a connection.

The storm blew eastward. Mr. Gilbert's lyrics were a few miles and tunes behind. She drove the expressway route, ironically cluttered with a stop light every hundred yards. Evening traffic was its usual congested self, and that was fine with me. The slower the better; it provided more car time with my teacher.

"Does rain have rhythm?" I asked.

"Hmmm. I guess it's what you make it. What do you think?" A simple question galvanized every nerve ending in me. It was the first time an adult asked me what I thought. My childhood had been spent being told what to think and never question it, what to do and what not to do, what to say and how to say it, and when I better damn well be quiet. Maybe it had been that way for the man who jumped from the bridge, maybe worse, and he couldn't take it anymore.

"I believe the rain always has something to say. Whether it's a whisper or a howl. We should take time to listen."

"What did the rain tell you today?" she asked.

"It said you can let me out where Franklin Avenue and Americus Street meet, two blocks from my house."

"You sure? I can take you all the way?"

"Yes, ma'am. Maybe one day you can take me all the way," I said.

"Please don't call me ma'am. I'm only nine or ten years older."

"Yes, ma'am. I mean yes, okay." Had there been a tailgate, I would have climbed and hid until the awkwardness subsided. Part of the ride, I spent in fear of her stopping in front of my house. Cars like hers rarely rode down Americus Street. To be seen with her was one thing. For her to have seen my house was another. I'd rather have gone another round with the Duke dog.

"You know, the day of the incident, I was walking to the office and thinking how college never prepared me for such a moment." We sat at the intersection and continued to talk. She seemed in no hurry to get home. "I kept wishing how I had my bike shoes on. I would have gotten to the office a lot faster."

"Bike shoes?" I asked.

"Yes, I love to ride."

"Me, too. But what happened when you got there?"

"I barged right in, straight to Father LaDuca's office. He was sitting at his desk with the school motto framed behind him." *Excelsior. Ever Striving. Ever Achieving.* The motto was a foreign concept to me, another mantra I was supposed to embrace while trying to conform to more rules and regulations. "First thing out of his mouth was, 'Don't you have a class?'" I pictured her standing there, explaining to a man with a partially bald dome, bushy flank hair, and a tightened tie which had turned his face red. "After I told him what had happened, he instructed me to salvage the rest of the class period and that he'd take care of it."

"That was it?" I asked. "He didn't ask how you were doing?"

"No."

I had imagined the closest LaDuca had come to a condom box was a public restroom. Men of the Catholic cloth held steadfast to the notion that condoms promoted sexual activity. Priests espoused their doctrine which advocated the proper rearing of boys.

"Most of us in class have a good idea of who did it. I was sworn to silence to keep it a secret, but I wanted you to hear it from me. Ronnie or Donnie. Maybe both. Two bullies who run together. I call them Pete and Repeat. I think one of them forced H. R. to put it there, or they definitely did it themselves."

"Thank you," she said.

"You're welcome. Thank you for the ride."

"Anytime."

The Montego taillights disappeared. "Anytime" gave me hope. Next time could not come fast enough. Getting home could not go slow enough. I mimicked the pace and the peace we used walking to the Montego. I replayed the last ninety minutes. The conversation.

The laughter. The music. Dancing while driving. Smiling in the rain. Our connection. Joy in slow motion. The shame of keeping her away from our house. I made my way home. Alone again, naturally.

CHAPTER 9

Weeks had passed since the Ronnie and Donnie show. I heard some song lyrics which described them when they hit the bricks running: "Like their asses were catchin' and their hair was on fire." Mrs. Wagenbach closed the condom case and never looked back. She settled into a routine, while I struggled with ninth-grade math and pimples.

"You're my kind of person," she said. She stopped the car at one of our "drop spots." The rides had become ritual. I should have sent Ronnie and Donnie thank-you cards since I had become the one student with a teacher chauffeur—and the best looking one in the school. The city. The whole state.

"How's that?" I asked.

"Because you love biking and swimming."

"And baseball and summer, too."

"Yes, I love summer, also, and I wish I could see you play baseball."

"Well, maybe you can. I'll try out in the spring for the freshman team. Maybe you can come to some games."

"Possibly, if I can get the paper load under control. What do you think about me starting a bike club?"

"Just tell me when and where, and I'll be there." The wheels and spokes in my head started spinning to bridges built long before I could cross them.

"Hey, what are you thinking about?"

"Summer of '72," I said. I stared at the floorboard. Fear had found an opening.

"Care to share?"

"The freedom of it. Holding on to a few more chances at being a kid," I said. I refrained from sharing what was truly on my mind—how next summer I'd be away from her for three months. "Bike riding to Mel Ott Pool. Baseball. The way a new ball looks and feels in my hand when I take the mound at dusk. The way the catcher's mitt looks, larger than a watermelon. My mom always sits behind the backstop. Sometimes, I'd choose which target to hit—her or the mitt."

"Not sure your mom's the type I'd want to tangle with. Try to focus on what's in front of you. Maybe we can find a way to do some bike riding and prepare us for what we do in the summer," she said.

Mrs. Wagenbach rested her chin on her left hand and her elbow on the steering wheel, smiling against the backdrop of a blue dress garnished with orange lilies. The stillness of her beauty was set with the impending sun, unceasingly secured to the horizon. It was an easy task to focus on her when she was in front of me and just as easy when she wasn't. But my joy was often balanced with agony whenever we went separate ways.

Each time I got out of the Montego, the same questions arose: what does she see in me that she does not see in other students? Why does she want to be friends? It was the quintessential mystery which haunted me, one difficult to answer considering I saw more deficiencies than good when I looked in the mirror. My self-esteem was several pieces of meat short of a po'boy—until it was lifted during our evening conversations. And maybe we were together because I was the only person who had come calling, including her spouse, when the rubber hit the road.

As a ninth grader, I had no answers to what swirled in my brain. Nor did I have questions directed toward the possibility we were doing anything inappropriate. I decided to let her "prepare for next summer" words direct my hope and imagination, words which filled my heart and drop-kicked fear to another planet. I headed to the corner store. The day was done.

*****

Our maiden voyage began with eleven easy riders at the foot of the Gretna Ferry. No helmets. One destination—Lake Pontchartrain. From fresh water to salt water. Mrs. Wagenbach scored permission from the principal and parents to organize Shaw's first, "unofficial" bike club. And she used the same tone prior to exiting the room the day the condom landed.

"Use the restroom on the boat. We'll be taking Jackson Avenue to Prytania where it meets at Audubon Park. Go no further. After we eat lunch there, we'll work our way to Canal Boulevard until it *T*s at the lake. I'll take up the rear, should an emergency arise."

"May I take up the rear with you, Mrs. Wagenbach?" I asked. Out of earshot.

"Yes, you may take up the rear," she said. I nodded then suggested the occasion should be officially blessed as "The Wheel Deal." The pun bloomed her double dimples.

I was the veteran ferry rider of the club—the only one whose grandmother lived on the New Orleans side of the river. When my Maw-Maw wasn't swinging a broom at Grandpa, she'd take David and me window-shopping along Canal Street. At lunch, she splurged for burgers and root beers at the Maison Blanche Fountain Counter. I walked in like I owned the joint—big cheese in The Big Easy.

The moxie I displayed at the store was sorely lacking when classmates were in the company of the teacher and me. It was a near everyday occurrence when I sat at my desk, listening and watching her teach. Being near my peers heightened my insecurity much the way silence did when I was in the company of the opposite gender. I sunk into a shell, fearing she would see them as smarter, funnier, better looking, and who lived in better houses.

My emotions overran any rationale—the fact that she was married and had much more than all of us was presumptuous of me to think they had something she wanted. At the same time, she had sent repeated, friendly overtures that she wanted to be with me.

Selfishly, I craved for the first off campus outing to be her and me, alone in the confines of the Montego, where I felt comfortable in my own skin. Yet, I either accepted the then present reality or have nothing at all. I was mired in frustration—where generating a conversation seemed Sisyphean, a task as tough as carrying books up Sue's steps. Most challenging was how to act and adjust in the moment. Richard the student or Richard the afterschool rider friend? And which, of the two, would she address? Or would it be both, depending how we slipped in and out of the moment? Having to play a dual personality as a fourteen-year-old was conflicting and complicated, especially for a boy who was having trouble playing with the one he had.

Pedaling eased my mind. Somewhat. On the first part of the journey, I stared at her legs more than I watched the road. She had worn her beloved bike shoes, which appeared to be a long-distance phone call from the bottom of her shorts. My mind went weak to that prurient place the day of the rescue, sans the stockings, and she smiled when she saw me looking.

Watching her glide along Prytania Avenue was good medicine. The street had history ridden all over it. Prytania had its share of oak trees and restaurants and paralleled iconic St. Charles Avenue. I worked up the nerve and asked if we could pay homage to a couple of landmarks: Prytania Theater and Lafayette Cemetery No. 1.

"Maybe we can one day, but we have to keep moving," she said. Unlike Gretna's Hook and Ladder Cemetery, No. 1 was diverse, housed with the Garden District wealthy and the Irish Channel working class, those who rode Mardi Gras floats and those who begged for beads. I took a final glance at the graves and acknowledged how death did not discriminate. And how "we," just her and me, might one day visit and get to stay for a long time.

The Garden District's opulence, decorated by Old Greek and Victorian mansions, arose to greet us as we halted at the pristine world of stillness and prosperity—Audubon Golf Course—hole number fifteen. Mrs. Wagenbach counted nine riders.

"I heard them say they were going to skip the park and head straight to the lake," D. W. said. He was a fellow St. Anthony student who lived on the edge of McDonoghville, where a person could stand on his porch and expectorate into the river. "But I thought they were kidding." D. W. was known for his wit and for his propensity to take little seriously. Our teacher was faced with a huge decision—eat park concession food or continue to the lake.

"We'll head to concessions. We have fifteen minutes to eat. So, order fast and eat faster," she said.

I had thought Ronnie and Donnie had moved on down the line, but two more followed in their footsteps. Ray C. had been one of B. J.'s cronies who feigned courage when surrounded by the St. Anthony bullies. At Shaw, he hung with Stevie P., a kid half his size but was twice the prankster. Twelve miles north, they sat on the lake steps laughing, while asking what had taken us so long.

The teacher kept her composure, politely explaining their bike days were over. She lectured about responsibility and safety and how their parents had entrusted her to their well-being. After future bike excursions, I came to realize the profound ambiguity in that statement.

The return to the morning's starting gate was long and lethargic, a group of tired, hungry boy bikers wanting nothing more than to be home. Except one. I would have ridden a hundred more miles for one of her smiles. When we reached the ferry, a fierce storm and chilly winds greeted us. Mrs. Wagenbach instructed me to stay near her once the boat docked on the Gretna side.

"Okay. The group bike trips are over. From now on, it's just you and me, buddy," she said. I thought I had water stuck in my ears. Mrs. Wagenbach's news lifted a heavy consternation from around my neck. Outside of school, she and I had become a company of one as long as she offered to ride me home. And she kept offering.

"Sounds like a real wheel deal," I said.

She managed to muster a soft smile. Almost as big as mine.

*****

She reneged. "A few parents, a few boys, excluding present company, and admin encouraged me to give the bike club another try," she said. "Encourage," within education, she noted, was synonymous with a "little pressure."

"Really?' I asked.

"I agreed only if they got a male faculty member to help. Brother JK volunteered. I wanted to share it with you first."

"Mr. Exactly?"

"You call him Mr. Exactly?" she asked.

"Yep. Every time he agrees with something, he says, 'Exactly!'" I said. I did my best Brother JK impersonation to impress her. "And he's got a case of the 'xactlies."

"What on earth is that?"

"His breath smells 'xactly like his butt!" The punchline brought a laugh and a smile.

"You need to go to confession," she said. Though Mrs. Wagenbach polished the bad news, she shared it in confidence, placing me ahead of others. Her tone was sincere and had a way of making me feel important in her life, something more than being a teacher's pet. "Would you like to know where the next bike adventure takes us?"

"No. Keep it…"

"Telling you anyway. Next ride comes to my house, and I'll feed everybody. Whattya think?"

"I agree. You should feed everybody. It'll be a longer trip, right?"

"Yes. About ten miles longer than the last one. Twenty-five miles one way. It may take four or five hours for the group, a little less if someone were riding solo." Something deep down said "solo" was a subtle hint. Something deeper convinced me to run with the pack and hope to one day go alone. But I had to be careful not to take her words for anything more than face value. It would have been easy for me to have crossed bridges yet built. I had to avoid speculation—a tall, Texas task for a kid whose emotions were seated on his sleeves.

The Algiers Ferry landing was preceded by cobblestone streets constructed by slaves purchased by their masters directly from barges—those who had been forced from their families and homeland and whose work had been reduced to modern bikes, cars, and shoes—everyday rubber rolling with the river.

I had sat on my three speed atop the landing, looking across the river at the St. Louis Cathedral. I questioned how something that beautiful on the outside had felt ugly on the inside of me—made worse knowing Brother JK was leading the ride while she awaited at home. A couple of paddle steamers were docked a short distance from its doors. Shoeless folk sat on the levee's grey rocks, soaking in Saturday's sunshine. I left the view and biked down the ferry ramp, leading our group to the boat.

"Park dem bikes near de lifeboat," a ferry worker said. He pointed his finger toward a bike rack adjacent to a boat the size of a pirogue. The captain sounded the 8:00 a.m. departure horn, and the engines rattled the iron deck and my teeth and bike. Other workers—covered in scowls, tattoos, and orange jumpsuits—released the hemp from the capstans. The propellers churned through the black water and pushed the boat to the Canal Street side.

"You think they can hit dat mooring?" D. W. asked.

"Dead ringer, bro. They could probably hit it in their sleep," I said.

"Just as long as dey hit it when dey awake," he said. The boat drifted, until the current guided it to the dock, when a rope took flight, landing silently. I saluted D. W.

Tourists and traffic made navigating difficult through the French Quarter, the city's oldest neighborhood. More challenging was getting past the aroma of café au lait and his brother beignet—a Café du Monde fritter smothered in powdered sugar. The coffee was the perfect liquid to wash down my favorite donut. Each swallow prompted pause, a moment of silence and gratitude.

To get beyond the sweet smell, I had created a mental diversion by giving our bikers and bikes labels. D. W. was *Desire Within*. Others were *Wild Mouse, Po Boy, Cool Handle Luke, Two Lane,* and *Fightin' Tiger* to name a few. I was *Smoky Mary*, in honor of Elysian Fields Avenue, the longest stretch of road running from Esplanade Wharf to Pontchartrain Beach. Little did I know that months to come an illegal "Smoky Mary" would greet me each morning and tuck me tightly at bedtime.

We moved through old Gentilly, Mrs. Wagenbach's middle-class neighborhood, where she lived until she finished college then took her marriage vows. She once drove me to her childhood home. I sat staring at its whiteness, a shell's throw from Shaw rival Brother Martin, another all male Catholic high school. Their driveway was ten minutes from St. Joseph's, her all-female high school. Catholicism had permeated every part of our parochial culture and had become one of our delusional bonds.

When we reached the Pontchartrain Amusement Park gates, Mrs. Wagenbach was waving and smiling. "What took you so long?" she asked—the same question Ray C. and Stevie P. had posed a half a mile from where we were sitting on our bikes.

"Hey! Mrs. Wagenbach! Fancy meeting you here," said Brother JK. He acted coy about the arrangement, while I remained in the background, expressionless, wondering why she had kept the surprise shrouded in secrecy. She outdid Mr. Exactly by staying upbeat and pretending everything was okay.

As we rode toward her house, I felt idiotic about the thoughts and the straight face I maintained. I felt worse about the way I looked at her and the animosity I felt. After all, she could have stayed home and graded more papers. But, then again, I thought, maybe, just maybe, she was there to see me.

I questioned how something that beautiful on the
outside had felt so ugly on the inside of me.

7333 Ligustrum Drive, located in what was then known as Kenilworth,
was a NOLA East suburb white flight development. The landscape
was cloaked in spec houses designed for young, up-and-coming pro-
fessionals, the newly married with aspirations of raising children away
from the racial divide. Nestled between I-10 and Lake Pontchartrain
and adjacent to water in every direction, the bedroom community
seemed sleepless and everything opposite Gretna.

Her house smelled and looked newer than the new Montego
parked in the driveway. Carpeted and hardwood floors. Spit shine
appliances. Climate controlled heat and air. Living room and bedroom sliding doors, minus the caution tape seen on the Shaw slid-

ers. A few open spaces awaited furniture, but she made the house a quaint abode, comfortable and inviting. And she had company.

The modernity scene of boys being boys listening to Top 40 hits while gorging on a smorgasbord of chips, dip, and fruit was overshadowed for me by Val, the Mrs. husband. He was a clean-cut, conservative looking guy, who spoke in a friendly, gentle way and made feeble attempts at humor. Other than Mr. Exactly, he owned the shortest hair in the house, a '50s' style, counterculture to the longhaired, freaky people of the '60s and '70s—and the high school boys who had overtaken his house.

I spent too much time "sizing him up," racking my brain as to how someone like *him* could get someone like *her*. I pictured Val having had the perfect life, free from hardship and how he must have sailed through school onward and upward as the model student and acclaimed valedictorian. How he had been most popular on campus as a male cheerleader, tennis player who married the most beautiful girl in my world and how he was the luckiest person in his world. I was beginning to love and dislike myself at the same time, a cocky kid with much less to give than what he thought he truly had.

"You guys will be as tired as a two tired bicycle when you get home," Val jokingly lisped. I feigned a smile. Unlike his wife who kicked him in the rear of his plaid shorts, as we straddled our seats for the return trip. Maybe she thought nobody was looking. But I was that nobody, who was always looking, because she told me it made her smile whenever I did.

CHAPTER 10

The last day of my first high school year had arrived. Along with it came the anticipation of my final ride with the teacher, and the pain of a potential separation was palpable. I had become a teenager who lived with one eye on the present and who feared the future with the other, and the recent past seemed like neither. The laughter and music, the bikes, and the conversations—all of it, I was certain, would vanish once the car door closed.

"Well, you sure were quiet today," she said.

"Yeah. Guess there's not much to say except good-bye," I said. Mrs. Wagenbach knew what was on my mind. I only knew what I *hoped* was on hers, but I dared not ask about the summer of '72.

"Try to stay positive. You have your restaurant job. Swimming. Baseball. Biking. All the things you love," she said. Biking struck a nerve, since she shelved the bike club again. I wondered if she'd keep her word and start anew in the fall.

"Yeah." I had one shoe on the floorboard and one on the concrete. Each foot felt caught between two worlds: the new, where I felt alive; and the old, where I simply existed. Both had pulled simultaneously in different directions. A year's worth of school materials and uncertainty weighed me down, and my emotions exceeded my ability to think.

"It'll be okay. I'll go out of town for a week or two. When I return, I'll spend time with my family in Gentilly, mostly with my parents. Other than that, it's the McKeaver dog and me."

"Going alone?" I asked.

"No." An awkward silence ensued. "Look. Try not to treat it like a funeral." Death was an appropriate analogy—her, the casket, slipping away into a tomb, and me, helpless to do anything about it.

"I'll try, but thanks just the same," I said. I saw our friendship in front of me and returning to the neighborhood gang was far less appealing.

"For what?"

"Your time."

"Hey. The year finished better than it started. I'm looking forward to the next one," she said.

Her car door had the sound of a hearse gate closing. I thought how the dead should be glad they could not hear.

*****

Berdou's Restaurant left a taste in my mouth exceeded only by summer biking, baseball, and swimming. And with good reason, it built a temporary wall between me and the teacher. A buck twenty-five an hour plus tips also helped. The job taught me work ethic in a customer-driven occupation relentless in serving and satisfying.

The French cuisine eatery was three blocks from my house and a half a block from the bridge. I often feared a station wagon crammed with kids would plow through the reedy rails during the middle of my work shift. My hope was to have been clutching one of George Berdou's entrees—one which made mouths water and placed customers' minds on a permanent vacation from their temporary woes. I discovered a similar feeling without lifting a fork one Saturday night.

"Richard, you have a phone call. Try to make it short," said Ida Berdou. Idea Ida, whom I dubbed for her business acumen, had a heart the size of the Natchez riverboat and ran a tight ship. She religiously locked the doors at 7:30 p.m., no matter who knocked—priest, pope, or president.

"Hello?"

"Hello, Richard?" My friend's voice, which had spoken a hundred hopes into my heart, came over the phone line.

"Ah, Richard doesn't work here anymore," I said. My heart had jumped to keep company with my Adam's apple.

"Well, when you see him, please tell him that Naomi called."

"Mrs. Wagenbach? Wait. This is Richard. I was...uh, just kidding."

"Yes. I know it's you, kiddo, and it's the summer. So, please call me Naomi."

"Ah, yes ma'am. I mean, sure."

"I've been out of town, and the time away gave me time to think. I realized I miss talking with you." The temporary wall came crashing down. Mrs. Ida gave me the "this is a business phone" look.

"Sorry, but I have to get back to work."

"Oh, I hope I didn't get you into trouble. Call me if you want. My number is 472-4722. I'm home most of the day, but if Val answers, ask for Mrs. Wagenbach."

I was confused when and where to use her first or last name; it was a trick, which would require practice. But I was sure of the voice on the other end of the phone which had mesmerized me, the mind which taught me and the smile that had brightly painted my world. Our friendship was naturally and beautifully evolving. Still, the questions remained: why would a married lady want to be friends? What did she want from me? What did she see in me?

*****

"Would you like to go to the lakefront with us?" The lakefront to locals meant Lake Pontchartrain, an oval-shaped estuary named for the French politician, Louis Phelypeaux, comte de Pontchartrain. The "us" included McKeaver, her white terrier who panted in the rear seat and wore a black *fleur de lis collar*.

"Is this the official Saint's mascot?" I asked.

"The one and only."

"Is Sir Doggie car-trained?"

"Yes!" Naomi smiled.

"Well, at least two of you are," I said. I refused to tell her that my bladder would go into overdrive whenever I was nervous. When I stepped into the car in front of the church where the priest and I had boarded the limos, I could barely breathe. And although it was June, I knew there were too many sets of eyes capable of seeing a student with his teacher.

"Think you can hold out until we get there?" she asked.

"McKeaver! You think I can hold out?" He looked at me with eyes too large for his head. He smiled, too.

A gentle wind pushed the waves toward us. About a mile as a pelican flies, cars rolled along Causeway Bridge. Men tended to fishing rods and crab nets scattered across the lakefront wall steps. Naomi and I sat on a bench under a baby oak tree. McKeaver held steady to his leash, while I felt free from mine—the confines of home, church, and school. The summer breeze liberated my mind and grounded me in the moment, even as I pinched myself for having been there. Me of all people. With her of all people.

"What's your dad like?" Naomi asked. I took the question as a conversation starter. It snapped me from glancing at a tan line across her back, revealed by a strapless halter top.

"My dad. Hmmm. No one has ever asked me about him. Well, he never met a stranger and a beer he didn't like. He always says OP beer is his favorite."

"OP?"

"Other people's beer. The free kind. Most nights, he sneaks one or two out of my mom's eyesight. Maybe he drinks to take the edge off," I said.

"What edge?"

"I guess six children and my mom whom he's always arguing with. Maybe it's his job. He works at Boutte's Machine Shop on Chef Highway. Not far from where you live. Most days, he takes the Algiers Ferry, then catches a bus to get there. My mom had to take a job with the public school board, so we can go to Shaw and my sister can go to Archbishop Blenk. I don't think he makes enough money to cover the tuition, unless they let poor people in. I don't know what goes on behind closed doors."

"Really? You think it's a Catholic thing?"

"Just as sure as that lake is wet. Religion rolls off my mom's tongue like those waves rolling into the wall steps, full of spit and a crash landing. And I think my head is like that wall." Naomi laughed a smile into the sun. Her face had a way of calming me, a face which could launch a thousand new shrimp boats. "But sometimes I think there is more when it comes to my dad," I said.

"Such as?"

"He fought in World War II, a nose gunner on a B-24 Bomber. He flew thirty-five missions. Watched planes go down, when his kept returning."

"That had to be hard. Seeing people die."

"Yeah. While he was in France, he got news that his best friend died when the parachute he was wearing failed to open during a combat drop. But what I admire about him is that he was raised through the Great Depression, the same time his dad was killed in a river barge explosion. My grandpa was laid out in their Harvey home. The same home my dad was born in."

"Wow. You think he went to war to escape all that?" she asked.

"I don't know. I never asked. I'm not sure why you'd leave one hell to go to another. His generation went to war, because they thought it was the right thing to do. Perhaps it was because of his brother which pushed him over the edge."

"What about his brother?"

"When he was twenty-one, he fell from a scaffolding and ruptured his spleen. He died a week later. My dad was just a young teenager like me. My dad was close to his brother, the way I'm close to David."

"I couldn't imagine losing my brother at that age," she said.

"I've tried to pick which affected him most, but when it comes to my dad, I know which experience affected *me* the most," I said.

"And what is that?"

"You remember Christopher Columbus' three ships?"

"Not really. I'm not as good with history as I am with English, although they sometimes overlap, and they both teach us."

I explained in vivid details about the drawing incident, the bruises, cuts, welts, and the pain. Perhaps, I continued, it was the war or his friend in France. Maybe it was the deaths of his dad and brother and the Great Depression. Perhaps it was my mom's constant nagging about drinking a beer. Maybe all of it came to a head, and he was a B-24 bomb, exploding each time the belt branded beneath my skin. I shared with her the doc's diagnosis—worst beating he had ever seen.

"What was your dad like when you were growing up?" I asked.

"I never could please him. No matter what I did, my best was never good enough. It's still that way," she said. "Guess it'll be that way until one of us dies." Naomi sat pensively, staring at a sailboat anchored several waves away, as the dog slept under the bench.

"My parents never held me to a certain standard. They only encourage me to do the best I can. My dad reminds me to find work I like, so one day I won't have to shovel shit in Louisiana."

"Would you like to look at my yearbook?" Naomi asked. It was a conversation changer—breaking the stillness and clearing the cloud, which saturated the conversation.

"What yearbook?" I asked.

"The yearbook when I became homecoming queen." Her voice faded into the wind as she walked to the Montego and grabbed a volume the size of Sue's books combined.

"You were a homecoming queen in high school?" I asked.

"College. The very first at LSUNO, but it was no big deal." The university resided on the lake's south shore, wedged between a canal and Elysian Fields and across from the amusement park.

"Why didn't you go to LSU in Baton Rouge?" I asked.

"I wanted to stay near my neighborhood. Home seemed like a better fit." As she turned the pages, I thought she could have won at the larger university, also.

"Who is this guy?" I asked.

"The SGA. The student government associate."

"Elaine. Naomi. Evelyn. Diane. Cathy. Lynn. Shirley…," I said, holding an imaginary microphone. Eight ladies stood on a makeshift stage strategically erected in front of the library. They smiled and waved to the mostly male crowd. "Oh! Look at you! There's Naomi!" Except for the obligatory cheerleader, each contestant wore a dress or a skirt.

Naomi stood with her hands on her thighs and had her left foot planted behind the right, forming a "T" pageant pose. She epitomized loveliness. Deep dimples. The curls of her '60s' hairdo kissed the corner of her mouth. A vote McCarthy button was pinned below her right shoulder. Her sleeveless pullover clung to her chest, creating a distinction for judges partial toward the well-endowed. Smart lady.

After a thrilling club football victory against Fordham University, Naomi accepted her crown. Cameras flashed. Cheers erupted from the podium. The pep band played the alma mater as she held roses and paraded around the gym with Mr. SGA. She danced until the school's president closed the ceremony. *Queen Naomi's Rein Commences* caught my eye as she shut the book.

"I know a place that has great snoballs. Would you like one?"

"Do they have chocolate with cream?" I asked.

"We'll find out."

"Why is there no 'W' in snoball?" I asked.

"No idea. I'd just chalk it up to our Newallins culture," she said. We talked until we arrived at the snoball stand, mostly about what we had looked like as kids. She had to dig deeper in time than me. I told her I would have thrown rocks at her house window from thirty feet away had I lived nearby.

On the return to the church, my head and sweetened teeth hung out of the window. The wind slapped my hair against my ears. I relived the day—the lakefront, McKeaver, the boats, the laughter and the stories, the yearbook, the chocolate and cream snoball, and her smile. And my smile—as we rode the bridge crossing smoky water, cotton clouds within my reach, wrapped in the ecstasy of freedom and the reality of not having to wait until September to see her again. Me, of all people, riding with the schoolteacher. Me, a boy of summer, riding with the queen.

*****

City Park, sister to Audubon Park, was an oasis dressed in a plethora of old oaks and magnolia trees. Ancient bayous ran through the heart of it. Art, food, music, and more attracted locals and tourists from near and afar.

After several trips to neighboring Lake Pontchartrain, Naomi decided to make City Park an additional place to visit. Geographically, it was the halfway point between our two houses and an easy bike ride for me—cross the Algiers Ferry, through the Quarter, straight up Esplanade, and into the park.

"I love this park, and I like this boat," Naomi said. Her hand had glided along a rental, sitting behind the concessions building, a Café du Monde replica. "Better to be in a boat than watching 'em from the lake wall." I pushed the boat from the shore and rowed parallel to City Park Avenue. The current and Naomi's natural beauty sparked a bit of boldness in me.

"Has anyone told you that you're a good-looking lady?" I pulled the oars up and let the boat glide.

"People have, but that's not important to me," she said. "Is someone being good-looking important to you?"

"No. You're born whatever you're with. I know people who think it's a big deal, but I try not to be like everyone else." I told her about Sue, Debbie, and others, girls I had a kid crush on, how I wanted to rescue people and to be fiercely loyal. And how they smiled in my "cute" face and used me.

"You're the consummate Pisces. Females rarely say what they mean or mean what they say. Some are just downright mean," she said. "And you're not like everyone else."

"How's that?"

"Well, you're an athlete who loves English lit, and your writing is above ninth grade level. You're the only ballplayer who has that

90

unusual combination. You're kind, quite humorous, and a great listener. And for what it's worth, you are very handsome. I keep wanting to see you, because…you're just you."

Her compliments stirred the water and the wind. I saw nothing, but sundrops on her face, luminous and resplendent. My mind drifted to dreams of time together, floating from a friendship to forever sailing in a tunnel of love.

"Well, if I am just me, why do the girls I like are always liking someone else?" I asked. I listened to her requited and unrequited love lesson and tried to make sense of it.

"One day, somebody will be lucky to have you. Never settle for something or someone less than what or who it is you truly want. But for the moment, we can enjoy our time together," she said. Naomi's face had the look of what she described—she had settled for less but could not bring herself to speak it.

She had rarely mentioned Val's name nor why or when they married. Maybe she had caved to parental and societal norms and pressures—get a degree, get a husband, get a job, get a home, and get busy in the bedroom. But I do know that Val was lucky; and if he could have such fortune, so could I. Fortunate enough that it would be someone like her and naïve enough to think it might be her. Maybe those were dreams of a pubescent boy whose feet were watered down in a wishing well.

We coasted through the tepid air, until the channel ended at Marconi Drive. Large oaks stretched their arms, and their rooted, gnarled toes were submerged in the black bayou. The tips of their mossy hair skimmed the water's surface. City Park was the sibling summer breeze, which had whisked our faces at the lake, with the McKeaver mutt sometimes at our feet.

"You see the swan?" Naomi asked.

"Yeah."

"The long white neck? It seems so sacred and gorgeous."

"Yes, it is," I said. Her words hung on my heart. As did her dark hair, white pants and her outstretched legs. Thunder rolled in the distance. "Yep. Sacred and gorgeous."

CHAPTER 11

Summer had moved at a fast pace, and I had worn our lake and park days everywhere I went—breakfast, biking, swimming, lunch, supper, on the pitcher's mound, and into the night when I counted stars in Naomi's eyes. Each morning I awoke, I hit the road running, but on days when we were getting together, my feet never touched the ground. We had become two parallel bridges stretching time and distance across the muddy Mississippi.

"I'm going to the pool, Mom. After that, a few of us will play some Home Run Derby at the park," I said. I had stuffed my swimsuit and glove into a towel and had once again told my mother a half-truth while tying my shoes. I convinced myself that a white lie was "having a plan."

"Okay. What about lunch?" my mom asked. She was doing what she did best—cooking. A spatula was an extension of her arm. She was either knocking down red beans and rice, shrimp stew, seafood gumbo, crawfish pie, fried chicken, potato salad, or dirty rice. I didn't wait around long enough to let the smell determine which.

"I'll think about it later. Tips were good at work the other night, so I can stop at the BK Lounge."

I pedaled to the church and parked my bike behind a rundown storage shed—reminiscent of ours but blessed with two floors and twice the trash. The shack was forever a sixth-grade reminder of where and when my buddy, Boyd, had asked if I wanted to see his sister's vagina. I had never heard the term "vagina," but by the process of elimination, I figured she could only hide two things while wearing her Catholic uniform. Up went her skirt. Down went her panties.

"You want to touch it?" Boyd asked. "She lets me all the time. It's wet and mushy."

"I thought you said, 'See it?' Nah. Better not." I was uncertain if a brother was permitted to touch his sister's vagina, but I walked away knowing girls would look identical if you stood them on their heads while they were naked.

"Ready to swim?" Naomi asked. I plopped into my Montego spot.

"Like a Pisces," I said. "I like your hair. Kind of looks like the lady on *Gilligan's Island.* You know? The one who always wears pigtails."

"Yes. Did you know that the lady who originally auditioned for the part was named Naomi McCarthy?"

"You auditioned?"

"No, but I tell people it was me, just to grab their attention," she said.

"Oh, kinda like a twin sister thing," I said. I pictured Naomi and Boyd's sister standing on their heads. "I'd tell everyone you look better than the one who landed the role."

"Thanks, little buddy."

"You can call me Skipper," I said.

A singer on the radio crooned how someone had made him such a happy boy, which described my condition at the time. Naomi did her shoulder dance. We crossed the bridge and headed toward the deep end.

We struck up a conversation about lake swimming. Naomi said she'd never put a toe in the water, but she would gladly sit with me all day at the wall. She clearly remembered in '68 when Lake Closed signs were posted, but some people still ignored the pollution warnings.

"Only hippies and dippies got in," she said.

"Dippies?"

"Hippies who skinny-dipped."

"Skinny-dipped?" I asked.

"Oh…um…people who swim naked."

"Far out. What kind of pollution?"

"Probably raw sewage and other crappy contaminants," she said.

I wondered if people and fish who fornicated had been on the list. "Like crappy naked people?" I asked.

"Like naked people," she said.

We walked through the pool gates and were greeted by blue water, a striking contrast to the brown lake. I instantly felt uneasy being with my shirt off. Was I too skinny? Was I muscular enough? Should I have stayed in the car? Questions concerning my masculinity, or the lack thereof, ran rampant.

"I love the pool, but I'd prefer an ool," I said.

"An ool?"

"Yes, a pool with no P in it. Which is where I'm going right now."

When I returned, Naomi was neck-deep in the water, and I was neck-deep in sunscreen and struggling to cover unreachable places. I saw the *Zephyr roller coaster* in the distance, then turned to watch Aphrodite in a two-piece rise from foam. Liquid cascaded from her skin. She climbed the steps at a snail's pace—a celestial scenery seventy times more picturesque than seven setting suns. I did my best to avoid looking like a teenager mired in horniness, but nature was having a hard time cooperating.

"Having a hard time?" she said.

"Very." I turned away, embarrassed.

"May I help?"

"Please. Thank you."

"My turn. Let me dry off," she said. Her high hips were perfectly curved, and her breast dipped tightly into the swim top. The cool water and the lakefront wind pointed her nipples upright. I played connect the dots on her freckled shoulders. Naomi giggled with each description of my intricate artwork and sighed as I massaged the white cream deeply into her pores. East, west, north, and south to the edge of her spine, until my fingers grazed her athletic cheeks.

"Looks good," I said.

"Feels good." She stepped against what I had tried desperately to hide. "Let's get in."

My hands and mind shook. I tried to process the flirtatious moment. Arrows and loose language had pointed to the possibility of our relationship becoming physical—a compliment here, subtle hints and music to encourage it. Maybe that's how first touches were supposed to have been, instinctive and startling—caught unaware and captured in vulnerable time. Maybe it was just a misstep on an adult's part.

The erection. A heat-seeking missile. A teacher with her finger on the trigger. Neither of us spoke a word about it. Not that day. Not even when we frolicked in the shallow end, taking turns swimming between each other's legs, wondering aloud what we'd eat for lunch.

*****

Football was soon to begin where summer had ended. Time with Naomi and our sensuous swim had occupied spaces between my ears. I had given her so much airplay that athletics had become an afterthought, until a car stopped in front of the church and evicted me from my castle in the sky.

"Heard you could chunk a football pretty good," said Coach Jennings. He stopped his Oldsmobile where I was awaiting the homecoming queen. I wondered if he had heard it from my cousin, who once informed me that I could hit a gnat's ass at two hundred yards.

"Yes, sir. I guess."

"Well, why don'tcha play? Was told you could chunk it a country mile and that you were real accrit," he said. I leaned against the driver door trying to understand his accent and block his view. I started sweating bullets, stupefied for a sensible explanation why a female and fellow faculty member was picking up a student during the summer—a married female, in front of God's house. "Think about gittin' yo ace out thar, son. We could use 'nutha quarterback."

"Yes, sir. I have been thinking about it. I really didn't like that I got very little playing time as a freshman. And that was at cornerback. They never gave me a shot at quarterback." In addition to acting, my purpose for being on earth was to play baseball and football. I wanted both sports to be my most significant high school experience, but along came Naomi. She did what no ball or bat could.

Coach Jennings adjusted his baseball cap on his football head and pushed down his cheap sunglasses. "I'll talk to the coaches. You let me know, boy," he said and drove away. Sixty seconds later, Naomi arrived.

"You look uneasy," she said.

"Very. Coach Jennings just drove away. He came out of nowhere."

"What did he want?" she asked. Her eyebrows pinched her nose, a thousand thoughts seemed to have thundered through her mind. We shared a tacit anxiety about "being seen," like we had been hiding something neither could describe, something yet to have transpired. It was as though guilt knocked and entered the backdoor.

It never occurred to me during my youthful war between euphoria and hormones that Naomi had everything to lose—her marriage, her home, her job and future jobs, and her reputation. I could not think in consequential or sinful terms no more than I could predict where our relationship was headed. I simply trusted her to make the correct decisions. She was my teacher.

"He wants me to play quarterback," I said.

"I figured that was only a matter of time, Richard." Naomi never much spoke my first name, but when she did, it was to capture my attention. My name, in her voice, put my world on hold.

"Where are we going?" I asked.

"Maybe to lunch. Don't know." Naomi left me hanging. The day began nothing like the way summer was previously ending. For a moment, the warm lake and bayou winds had shifted in another direction.

*****

Bud's Broiler was dead center between a cemetery and the sidewalk on City Park Avenue. The diner specialized in charbroiled burgers, meat covered with hickory smoked sauce and grated cheese. Bona fide shoestring fries overloaded a plate and a stomach. Bud's opened the year I was conceived. Fate would have it that my first visit would be with the least likely person either side of the Mississippi River. Since high school, I have refused to visit certain places in New Orleans. The memory and the pain remain fresher than a Bud's Broiler bun.

"So, if I choke to death on a burger, they'll toss me out back?" I asked.

"If you choke, you'll die with a smile on your face," Naomi said. She sat with her back to a window—blue shorts, loose V-neck shirt, knees up, flip-flops on a bench—cute like a girl, pretty like a lady.

"Are you saying I'll eat only one? And I'll die smiling because yours is the last face I'll see? I have wondered if lovers buried together might embrace for eternity." I remembered how we rode bikes past Cemetery No. 1, thinking romantically that she and I might one day spend a long time there.

"The Tristan and the Fair Iseult story speaks of two branches which eventually intertwine," she said. Mesmerized, I listened to the twentieth century love triangle turned tragic by an intoxicating love potion, as the jukebox played our favorite songs. I was lost in a trance when a middle-aged man dressed in cook's attire notified us that our order was ready.

"If you decided against playing, Richard, you can still ride with me after school," she said. Naomi waited for the right moment to alter the conversation and return us to football. And to the future. "Do they practice on Saturdays?"

"I think varsity players meet in the morning to watch film from Friday night's game." My first Bud's bite transported me to paradise, without choking.

"That doesn't leave much time for Saturday," she said. "Saturdays are mostly free or as free as I make them. What do you want to do?"

"Are you saying that if I don't play, we will see each other on Saturdays?"

Naomi tried to hide her smile, then blurted a Brother J "exactly."

It was an excruciating decision, which required intense thought—Naomi's everyday car rides and Saturday bike rides? Or blood, sweat, and brain bashing on the gridiron? And what about baseball? Was I trading two temporary loves for a potentially permanent one? Trading pigskin for her skin? Throwing baseball leather for her lace? The beauty before me overshadowed football Friday's spotlight, although I had repeatedly cautioned myself not to cross a bridge before it had been built.

I felt insane to have been presumptuous. Yet, moments existed when her words and actions pointed toward something or someone more that she was not contently married to Val. Maybe *I* was the something or someone. After all, she was sitting with *me* in Bud's fuckin' Broiler! Not Val or another male, another student or faculty member from Archbishop damn Shaw—but with *me*!

"I'll punt football, Brother J 'exactly,' but your breath smells better," I said.

"What took you so long?" Naomi had a way of asking me questions with her laughing eyes.

"I try not to talk with food in my mouth."

"Easy burial, if you choke," she said. "And since we won't see each other as much as last year, we need to find a way to stay connected during school."

"Like what?"

"Don't know."

Naomi left me hanging for the second time that day, but it was the first time I had looked forward to school starting. I took the last bite of burger and listened to a song about two lovers meeting daily in the same café. I buckled my seat belt before getting back into the car.

CHAPTER 12

We played with fire. I held the matchstick; she held the box. I had been living in a "is this truly real?" world entering my second year at Shaw. And for whatever reasons, I still had a difficult time accepting what she had seen in me. It was though mystery ruled the day. Just as mysteriously, she further wanted to push the envelope, to play the duplicitous game. I decided not to push anything including the envelope. Yet, Naomi had an idea which could have burned us both.

"We both like to write, right?" she asked.

"Right."

"I considered this at Bud's, but it hit me later when we sat under our tree at City Park. I waited to tell you after I was certain it would work."

"Are you certain?

"Yes, as certain as I'll ever be," she said.

"Well, I thought you were Naomi." She threw a piece of wadded paper at me.

The plan was simple. The execution was precarious. No tools. No assembly required. Pick up the textbook containing a letter. Five minutes to beat the tardy bell. Read, respond, and return a letter in the same book by seventh period. Place the book where I found it. Repeat daily. It was like taking medicine, we just needed to be careful we didn't overdose.

We rehearsed as she drove me home, reminding me to be careful and creative. We discussed potential dangers and strangers who might get in the way. For each "what if," we sought solutions—always hand the book to each other. Write during quiz and test time. Always sit in the last seat. Cover the writing. The list went on. Naomi pulled age, rank, and seniority and wrote first:

September 1972

Richard,

Although I've told you how much I appreci-
ated you coming to see me after "the incident,"
our summer together has given me the desire to
write...

Our friendship has developed as naturally
as breathing. It's been an alluring and pleasing
experience...and I want more. In some way, it
feels inevitable...that we can make each Saturday
our day...

And thanks for the summer fun—the lakefront, City Park, the boat, biking, swimming.
You even make applying sunscreen fun...

Please know that I am here to help you
avoid any tenth-grade pitfalls...but it's difficult
to teach, when all I think about is YOU!

I look forward to your first letter!

Naomi

Writing was one of many vehicles she allowed me to employ without restrictions and judgment. Putting a pen to paper placed me on a pursuit of liberty, while tapping into a skill equal to sprinting, throwing, or hitting a ball. Letter writing also brought us to the real-ization that we had much to say, with not enough world and time to say it.

We had grown closer. Our friendship had remained genuine, one I daily depended upon. But a magnetic energy resided beneath the surface. The lightning bolt was charged and ready to strike and send me to a place I had yet traveled; it had become not a matter of "if" but a matter of "when." We both felt it. Occasional, temporary touches had been placed permanently on our minds—with words on paper to encourage it, propel it. Bikes. Car. Conversations. Dreams. Food. Swimming. Writing. Saturdays. Everything but October's embrace.

*****

October's Embrace

Storms had moved through the city two days prior to her birthday—gifting us a cool October Saturday. Unspoken ebullience filled the air. Adults played Frisbee and flew kites, while children chased squirrels. A man wearing sunglasses blew a sax on the New Orleans City

Park Art Museum steps. Most discernible was that lovers loved and laughed. Some pedaled boats across Bayou Oaks. Others walked hand in hand on the dense St. Augustine grass. It looked like a holiday.

Naomi had driven once through the landscape before setting the car on Le Long Avenue. I walked to our tree and looked across the bayou at a Christian school sitting at the edge of the bank. I wondered if it were coed and if the weekend walls and halls spoke in whispers about a student and a teacher like us. Same place. Same time. Same station.

"Boo!" Naomi said. Her finger poked into my ribs. I never flinched. "You don't scare easily."

"Only having my heart broken scares me."

"Let's go walking," she said.

"Yessa, boss." She poked me again.

We stopped at the Peristyle, a neoclassical pavilion, an elegant lady whose columns reflected in Bayou Metairie. "Couple's come here to pledge their eternal love," Naomi said.

"I'd change the name to Paris Style, where true lovers remain together until eternity is through," I said.

"That's romantic. You're a deep thinker for being so young," she said. We playfully bumped into each other.

"More like a deep stinker."

"Thinker, kiddo, and I'll hear of no other way."

"Yes, ma'am," I said. I moved too quickly for the next finger to reach my ribs.

"You better run."

"Are lions always at these structures because they are pavi-li-ons?" I asked.

"Good one, Mr. Herzog, but it's probably because lions symbol-ize strength and prudence."

"Prudence?" I asked.

"Being wise. Not to overdo certain parts of love. Maybe to keep an even mind and an overall balance." It was appreciative, prudence given to a simple boy.

"Sounds to me like prune juice or the prudence thing needs to lighten up and come out to play." I climbed upon the lion and jumped. Our eyes met. So did our hands. We walked toward a low, ashen wall surrounded by Ligustrum and morning glories racing to the edge. In that moment, I thought my life had begun.

"You can come closer," she said.

I slid until our blue jeans touched, and our fingers fit together. Birds hopped about, tweeting in their language. Clouds danced. The wind blew golden leaves to our feet. "Can you believe we are holding hands? I can barely breathe. I…"

"I can believe it. It's peaceful and comfortable. And I imagine it will get better," she said.

"You think it will?"

"I know it will," she said.

"Promise?" I asked.

"I promise."

"Now you're speaking Paris Style."

Naomi stepped onto a turn of the century carousel and straddled a flying horse. I looked for a lion but chose to stand by her side. Prudence. We circled back in time, surrounded by carved, hand-painted animals, stained glass windows, and a myriad of sparkling lights. It seemed like a magical meeting at night in the middle of the day.

"I think I'd be better going up and down than going around and around," I said.

"Why?"

"Motion sickness."

"Do the best you can. Focus on one thing," she advised.

"Okay. I'll stand directly behind your *behind*."

"That'll really make you sick."

Naomi smiled throughout the ride, then described the colorful carousel in theatrical terms, as we walked toward the car. I avoided nausea, but I had begun to feel the curtain closing on the end of the day. My body dragged, as though the impending sunset searched to steal my strength away. As though our impending going separate ways loomed, leaving me to stand alone in a fearful shadow.

"Let's walk to our tree where I tried to scare you earlier," she said. The edges of our hands hit until our pinkies braided, a peace promise which signified everything.

We sat where I had stood when we started our day. A tree root stretched between us. Naomi crossed her legs and leaned against the bark. I wrapped my arms around my knees. "Does this look familiar?" I asked.

"Hmmm…"

"This is how you sat at the burger joint," I said.

"Feels the same, too. Me on one side and you on the other."

I slid across the grass and fell into her October embrace. The cradle catapulted my shadow of fear ten thousand miles away, and our human touch had joined us with lovers who loved in the park. Had I a place to die, it would have been there, clothed in her arms.

I devoured the smell of her hair and shirt, as my ear pressed against her chest. "I can feel your heartbeat," I said. I matched the rise and fall of our breathing—a synchronized undulation. It was the beginning of the end of my innocence.

"Two hearts in harmony," she said. "Every day should be Saturday." I wanted the sound of her blood to echo in a place devoid of time. My finger inscribed across her sternum, as her "it will get better" promise planted in my mind.

"What did you write?" she asked.

"Our initials," I said. She brought her head closer, inches from my lips. I waited.

"And there they will stay, until eternity is through."

*****

While Shaw students were growing curious and asking questions concerning my relationship with a faculty member, only four people had truly known I had been "seeing" her. David, Perry, Billy, and Ray were blood and neighborhood brothers I ran with when I wasn't running with Naomi. A trustworthy understanding existed that what was said and done among us never left the shoes in which we walked.

After I hinted I had something monumental to reveal, they jokingly pressed me for details one February night. I was content keeping the mystery to myself, but I had grown tired of their teasing and challenging my teenage manhood. It was time to put my marks where her mouth had been.

"Come on, bra. Stop bullshitting us. Put up or shut up," Perry chided. We sat cracking peanut shells in Ruby Reds, a hamburger dive on Esplanade Avenue.

"Okay. Y'all ready to see this?" I asked.

"Damn!" David said.

"Holy shit!" Perry yelled.

"How did that happen?" Billy asked. He laughed with a cigarette dangling from his lips. Ray grinned and shook his head and sipped his beer.

Desire had reached an incurable fever since our October embrace had lit the fuse, which started the fire that boiled our blood. While I had kissed several girls, Naomi was the first woman whose lips had pressed against mine. But making out and caressing had elevated our emotions and frustrations with a shivering ratio, shooting skyward toward an envious sun. Desire had also tested Naomi's imagination.

I had unbuttoned my red flannel shirt and displayed the twenty-four hickey masterpiece she sculpted earlier that day. It was the closest I had come to starring in my own movie—being Bogart, black and blue bloodsucking leeches in *The African Queen*.

*****

"Take off your tie," Naomi said. My eyes had closed, and my mind had drifted to the rhythm of the rain pelting against the Montego. A damp December and relentless wet weather had forced us to put the bikes away. The city stayed saturated throughout winter and into the start of spring, enough for the Mississippi River to kiss the top of the levee. Enough to confine us to the car.

Naomi bypassed the "drop spots" on the neighborhood out-skirts and drove toward Algiers. Visibility was difficult. I had no idea where she was taking me, but since she had pinned me against the car door and performed her hickey artwork, I had an inkling why. I was confident she knew what she was doing, as she settled the car on a stretch of grass. The headlights faced the levee. The taillights faced Elmira Drive. We faced each other.

"Are you asleep?" she asked. "I said, 'Take off your tie.'"

"Oh, sorry. I was listening to the rain, which I happen to love. It sounds like hamburgers on a grill. Nobody would go hungry, if the rain tasted like burgers," I said.

"Is food the only thing teenage boys think about?"

"Not me. I think about listening to my teacher, especially a bossy one."

The sound of the rain disappeared when our noses and lips met, as well as our tongues. Naomi slipped me her gum, and I sent it back. She released a soft groan, unbuckled my belt and slacks, and slid her hand inside of my underwear. I trembled. "Are you nervous?" she whispered.

"Yes."

"It's okay. I'll lead you," she said. Her free hand changed the radio station to a tender tune about "the first time." And it was.

Roberta Flack flawlessly serenaded, "I knew our joy would fill the earth and last to the end of time." My heart "trembled" to the beat of a "captive bird."

She took my hand and placed it on her blouse button and appeared impressed by my dexterity, as I unfastened them one by one. Our tongues moved in harmony with the cellos, until we separated, and I received my first tutorial on bra unfastening. Although I had seen the *Playboy* photos, the pictures poorly compared to what would forever be emblazoned in my memory. My mouth met her erect nipple. I followed her lead and placed my hand softly into her pants and petted her pubic hair, moved my fingers south, and penetrated her warmth and wetness. Boyd would have been proud.

"Take off your shoes and pants," I said. The student had turned teacher. I threw one of my bold boat moments I had in the park, and she threw both to the rear seat. As an act of lagniappe, Naomi removed her yellow, cotton panties, too. The rain strands against the window highlighted her eyes and hair, which had fallen partially across her face—a perfect portrait—libidinous and sublime.

"Your pants. Off they go," she said.

"Make me."

"Gladly."

She placed her hands on my shoulders, guided me to an upright position, and straddled. The radio played another love song. She strummed my face, as her tongue found an erogenous spot. She made me.

"It's time," she whispered and placed me in her. "I love you."

It was March 6, a Tuesday with Naomi and five days prior to my sixteenth birthday. Not a condom box in site.

CHAPTER 13

Third period class had ended when I swung by her room to say hello. Naomi's grin accentuated a navy pullover covered by a brown leather jacket. A loose, black belt hung around her plaid pants. A few minutes prior to my arrival, she smiled for the camera, pegging another yearbook photo shot. No doubt the student photographer wore a smile, too, but not nearly as big as mine.

"Good morning, little schoolboy. Would you like to go to Texas today?"

"I'd love to go to Texas, my favorite state of mind and body," I said. "Can we read some Longfellow?"

We discovered "puttin' out road" with a street sign labeled Texas after vacating Brechtel Park in Algiers, a park one-eighth the size of City. Naomi had searched for something more secluded than the levee and places where people played, and we need not depend on the weather to cloud the windows.

"Yes, bring Longfellow. Meet me here after school, and try to control your smile," she said.

Early morning and my school day had been completed. I could not have been more art apathetic. History class was history long before it arrived, and a PE teacher told me to "wipe the grin from my face," as he checked attendance. *That's Mr. Grin to you oh-how-you-have-no idea-what-I'm-doing-after-school. And there ain't nothing better*, I sang from the corners of my heart. Hell, I didn't feel guilty during religion class. I heard little that day, save for her breathing in my ear, a windful reminder that we had traveled down Texas Road several times before.

*****

"Do you remember when we first held hands?" I asked. Her left hand had held the steering wheel, her right hand rested on the seat underneath mine.

"Yes, City Park. We were like two kids on a first date, wanting to touch but uncertain how to or if we should. Then it happened naturally."

I relived how she was the older kid and how we talked in the colonnade near the park Peristyle. A replica of ancient ruins was dressed in flowers and thickets. A square of hairy grass separated the wall, as we shuffled hand in hand. I spun her around as her laugh spilled into the October sky. Naomi described the amorous moment in a letter:

Richard,

My mind often returns to the time when we first held hands…an embrace which signified we were ready. Your hands were one of the physical gifts I noticed. Long fingers, dark skin, and protruding veins—strong but steady and slow and kind…

"Oh! Here's the new song I was telling you about," she said. "It sounds like Herzog, something to find." Her smile was wider than the windshield and the one I had worn earlier that morning.

"Yes, it does!" I played along, although the lyrics sounded like "hope for." Either way, in her eyes, it gave me my name and something to hope for.

She steered slowly onto Texas, a deserted stretch of street walled with weeds and bathed in broken beer glass. She parked midway between intersections—a routine she used to detect oncoming vehicles. Gray clouds and moisture had filled the air. A woodpecker in the distance hammered hard and fast.

"There are times when I have to pinch myself, seeing how far we have come, living this." Naomi had rotated her hips toward me and had taken hold of my hands. "It seems unreal, but I came to realize how I *thought* I felt like this before, when I'd been faking it. On the day I got married, it seemed like I was doing one more thing to please my father. I've been trying to please him my whole life. Then you came along."

It was the first time she had mentioned her dad since our first lakefront outing in the summer of '72. I never asked questions, nor did I press the issue. I figured she'd explain when she was ready, figured I'd listen, and let my silent lips do the talking. I leaned in and kissed her, pulled away, and sent a sympathy smile. She placed her hands to my ears, kissed the tip of my nose, then formed a wet clasp on my mouth.

Time froze, but it did not allow for a slow ride. Evening traffic loomed. I pulled the detached belt and made room to remove our shoes and pants. Time did not allow for full disrobing. Greedily, I pushed my hand under her pullover to touch her breasts. Our eyes met. Time did not allow for foreplay. A quick ride through Texas was on her mind.

My fingers skimmed smoothly past her knees to her ankles, where I gently pulled, and her head settled on the armrest. My touch reversed course and glided along her thighs, then fondled her until she was dripping and ready. She glanced. I was upright, twelve o'clock. Her countenance beckoned.

Our hips danced the Texas Two Step, quick, quick, slow, slow when she whimpered and sighed. Naomi clutched the back of my hair and implored me to orgasm. We sashayed in blissful rhythm, until I shuddered into her loins. Her breath had become a tsunami in my ear. The woodpecker had flown away, as rain tripped the light fantastic against the Montego window.

"Sex can be like going to the bank," I said.

"Really? How is that?" Naomi asked.

"Because once you withdraw, you can lose interest." She laughed and put her pants on. It was another stormy Monday. We sat in the Montego parked in the spot where I had lost my virginity. I watched a ship's smokestack pass by and glimpsed at pigeons finishing the remains of a stranger's lunch.

"But we don't have sex," she said. Curiosity covered my face. "*We*, Sir Richard, make love. Sex is selfish, more self-centered. Making love is other-centered, where two people simultaneously satisfy each other. Like we do."

"I love when the teacher teaches me. So, it brings you joy to satisfy me?" I asked.

"Yes, and I hope you feel joy, also," she said.

"More than I can describe. But how do I know if you are satisfied?"

It was a question I had thought about—me, a tenth grader trying to satisfy an older, more experienced person. With Naomi, I had lost my sexual innocence. And more. I had lost and forsaken the guilt Catholicism had imposed. To commit adultery and only feel her love meant I had also surrendered my soul, no longer caring about what was right and what was wrong. Naomi had become my moral compass, my heaven on earth.

Nor did I know, at the time, that she was committing statutory rape. And had I known the term, I doubt it would have stopped me. The power of her love had a tenacious hold on me. And I had assumed she was happy with me, unhappy in her marriage, and was going to help me escape my environment. But I never assumed that if she did this to Val, she would one day do it to me. At age sixteen, I was certain I was the one. Life and love loomed large.

"Well, I'm here, and I'm not going anywhere. I am satisfied before, during, and after we make love. I keep returning, don't I? Why do you seem so worried, Richard?" Naomi asked, as she rested the car against the Franklin Street curb.

"Not sure. I rarely see you during the day. It was better when I was in your class. Sometimes, I feel like an outsider. Do you *have* to leave now?" `

"Yep. Gotta get. Long drive and dinner to cook. Papers to grade. Thankfully, I have you to see tomorrow. Do you have homework?" she asked.

"Only what one of your fellow English teachers gave."

"How dare them? Mean English teachers. What's a poor boy to do?" From euphoria to dysphoria, in a matter of a few words, I sank. "I'm sorry. I only meant that figuratively," she said. During our park walks, I had shared what it was like to have been raised with little money and materials. She convinced me that we'd one day do well together.

"Yes, my family never had much. My mom took a job, so her children could have a Catholic education. The only part I've liked about that is you. You're the only reason I want to come to school. You're the reason I get out of bed. Heck, you're the reason I want to get in bed. While I know I can't buy you anything, I do want to spend all my time with you. All I have right now is love. And hopefully that's enough to..." words faltered through my tears.

"Enough to what?" she asked.

"Enough to buy more time, so I'll show you that I will make something of myself. And you can take that to the bank."

The next day, a morning letter awaited to greet me.

Dear Goula Boy,

How I enjoyed walking behind your goula this morning. It made me wish the day had ended... and I could put my hands on the goula I've come to know...Maybe we can go to Texas today, and I'll make things better. Promise. Please accept my apology about the "poor boy" comment. It was a "poor" choice of words! Ha! In no way did I intend to hurt you. Money or no money, I love you just the way you are—your humor, intelligence, your deep thinking, your good looks, and your ability to listen—the fact that you cared when no one else did. It makes me realize how rich-ard I am! (sounds like your humor)… Saturday is only a few days away.

I love you!

-N-

"You sure know how to make up as well as you make out, and last year's English teacher would have crucified me had I written without paragraph transition," I said. It was the second time I read Tuesday's letter, but the first time I had read it aloud, sitting next to her, as we sat at the corner of Franklin and Americus Street.

"Yes, you're right, but I'm too pressed for time. I try to capture my thoughts as they come down. Are you grading me?" she asked.

"There are not enough numbers or letters to grade you, ma'am."

We kissed long and hard. Not even air could slip between our sealed lips.

*****

Naomi's taillights once again disappeared toward the bridge. I noticed she had taken a different road, the same street the limo driver used to transport the priest and me to Mothe's Funeral Home, canals on one side, shotgun houses on the other. Death awaited between the two.

I gave little thought to it when I saw Perry signaling an SOS from a block away, waving wildly, as I carried my books, none of which I'd open for the remainder of the evening. The thought of Perry's older brother having used my friend's head as a punching bag was laid to rest when I noticed two shadowy figures behind him. Both were wearing shit-eating grins while standing next to an elderly lady. The levee and the river loomed large in the background.

"Hey! These two punks are harassing Two Teeth," Perry yelled.

It was customary that the louder he screamed, the further his glasses slid to the tip of his nose. The humidity contributed, forming sweat that flowed from his ropy hair, as cotton clouds lay motionless against the evening sun.

Two Teeth Melee had two gray protruding teeth and less than two cents to her name, which, regretfully, I never learned. She adorned her one tattered dress with split slippers that scraped the sidewalk. Her braless breasts freely swung from right to left, and she hunched more than Quasimodo. Wiry gray strands fell from a scalp covered with purple veins resembling a road map.

"Your mama sucks horsecocks!" she hollered, scratching the eczema on her arms. Quasimodo Eczemodo was the name I had secretly given her, a cryptic epithet I'd keep even if she were to die the next day.

A red mark the size of a silver dollar welted from her knee, compliments of one of the two bullying just to bully—inciting her to out-cuss any two-bit Bourbon Street whore. Perhaps she had grown tired of society's stones striking her, knowing nobody would answer her rescue call—tied to a lifelong pillory, the wheel rolling perpetually along. I know that I had grown exasperated from watching, simply being a bystander. The day I stayed to help console Naomi had given me the confidence I lacked to aid those in distress. "You motherfucking bastards! Come closer so I can piss on you!"

I was uncertain how she accomplished her daily outing. A sundial would have been handy to time her steps—a stiff limp that shuffled her from corner to corner, a respite from a house littered with cats and litter boxes. Perry surmised that Two Teeth had her fill of fur and scooping cat crap from containers she struggled to reach.

Presumed because neither one of us graced the inside of an abode which stood on toothpicks and prayers. Rags stuffed numerous window holes created by rocks. Weeds adorned the top of her porch, and the roof shingles had taken refuge in rusted gutters. The wood siding peeled as badly as her skin. It was as though osmosis had joined them as one, as though both summoned someone to scratch and coat their surfaces.

Nobody came.

"What bitch? Who you talkin' to, ho?" The skinnier of the two reached for another rock after taking offense about the verbal accusation thrown his momma's way. His shorter, wider sidekick stood watching with a smile and a waistline that exceeded his beltline. Equally worthless. He looked out the corner of his fat sunken eye. I had seen their type before, and I despised them.

"Hey fatty and skinny! You feel pretty big bullying a defenseless lady?" I asked. A scent of cinnamon had blown from the corner bakery, a store which had once sat on a select street until the Vietnam conflict had taken half of our neighborhood and most of its business.

"Dis ain't no lady. Dis a ho. We gonna beat dis bitch down! And who da fuck are you?" Skinny resembled a broomstick turned sideways—wide only were his high-top sneakers and shaggy socks. He stood shirtless with clenched fists, and a hint of fear crossed his no-'count countenance.

"Oh, oh," Perry said. A river freighter blasted its horn.

"I'm getting ready to show both you turds who I am." My school books found a place in the shadow of bodies. I noticed Two Teeth had worn only one house slipper. A torn toenail held steady to dangled yellow flesh.

"Come on. Let's go," Fatty told Skinny.

"I'm gonna take the thin one out first. If Fat Boy comes to his rescue, feel free to join…"

"Watch!" Perry…

I spun and swung at the call of Perry's voice, landing solidly to Skinny's jaw, whose teeth grinded against my knuckles. A right, left roundhouse landed on his ribs and stumbled Skinny to his knees. His partner in crime stepped into two jabs to his right eye. Fatty fell face forward. Skinny rose to his knees, turned tail, and ran.

Two Teeth Melee stared into my eyes and tottered away, mum. Perry and I shuffled home and gave no thought to the body that had lain behind, vanquished.

****

"Your brother's in bed," my mother said.

"In bed at four? I thought he got off of work at five or six. Is he sick?" I asked. I had stayed true to my after-school routine while trying to leave the thought of Two Teeth behind: books to the first available chair, rush to the refrigerator to grab the milk and cereal.

"No, he's not sick. He's just not well."

"So, why is he in bed?"

"Just leave him alone. He's in a lot of pain," she said. Tears formed in her eyes. Milk spilled to the side of the bowl.

"Pain? What kind of pain?"

"Just leave him alone!"

I deciphered her typical parental path of how issues were explained—many questions, no answers—sweep it under the rug. Ten and twenty years down the road, the truth would surface.

"How can I do that when we share a room?" I asked. A sliver of joy entered my heart, knowing I had finally inherited my own bed now that two of my other older brothers left the house.

"Be as quiet as you can, or I'll put the belt on you!"

"Good luck with that, Mom. I'm in high school. You ain't putting a belt across my butt anymore." I took my cereal to the room and neglected her the satisfaction of eye contact that would have prolonged another useless conversation.

David was covered in white sheets from head to toe in the dark. I recalled the time the Harbour Police fished a corpse from the river on a misty, damp December day. We had missed the ferry and had fifteen minutes to kill.

Over a railing, I saw an indistinguishable fleshy figure, steel stiff, its right arm frozen at ninety degrees. The joy of spending the last three hours window-shopping on Canal Street with our grandmother had vanished. I took three steps back as the passenger boat disappeared into a dense fog.

"Is that you, Rich?" David asked.

"It's me. What's the matter? Are you sick?" I kneeled next to my brother, ready to hear his final words and his breathing, which seemed to have disappeared into the placidness of the room.

"They're to-together every day. Jumped me. Fi-fi-five of them. Except Fridays. Only one stays late...bank clo-closes at...at six," David stammered. The rib pain burned each breath and choked his speech. He kept the sheets tightly tucked over his head.

"Real men, huh? Five against one," I said. My blood boiled. "You know I'll go after them." We were the "M&M Boys," Mantle and Marris, stitched tighter than a baseball, but we hit from opposite sides of the plate.

"No. They're too...too b-b-big fo-for you."

"Yep. That's what they told your namesake when he went after Goliath."

"Prom...prom...promise me you won't. They're not...not... not worth it."

I saw David twitch for the first time.

"Plus, I...I...have to wor-wor-work with them again."

Okay. Then why are you giving me all the details? Same thing I told Mom: good luck with that.

"I promise." Sometimes I had to lie to tell the truth.

I never personally knew the five, but their history was notorious. They had received a high school diploma the year before David graduated and were inseparable during their academic tenure—bank dicks who eventually posed as tellers. David had been the newcomer; perhaps they did not take too kindly to a younger, smarter boy who had drawn compliments from the management.

"Where are you going?" Mom asked.

"I'm going to the bank. And I'm taking Mr. Al Kaline." Twenty-nine inches of baseball bat I had used to spray baseballs around our hometown playground. Recompense.

"Oh no, you're not! I'll be damned if they'll beat you up too." Her face was as red as Two Teeth Melee's knee.

"Okay," I said. It had become my standard promise that I would or would not.

My mom got busy in the kitchen, an every-waking-minute habit that kept her occupied. No doubt she cooked in her sleep also. I pulled the banana seat-built-for-two bike out of our shed and cleaned

117

Mr. Kaline; David's painful stuttering echoed in my ears. Perry had a chance to drive should he decide to join my ride by.

For three evenings, we sat at the corner of Second Street and Newton Avenue, hiding behind a wall and surveying the landscape. The four-o'clocks inhaled, opening their faces to the world; exhaled, then bowed to the heat. Perry searched the perimeter on the last day as I white-knuckled the bike bars. Big bat Al waited for me back home—resting from the daily practice I inflicted on a duffel bag filled with river sand and hung from a shed rafter. Each swing landed on the miraged body of the bank boys, exacting screams and cries for mercy with every decisive blow.

"The same two exit the backdoors and get into their vehicles," Perry said.

"Every day except Friday."

"Whaddya think?" Perry asked.

"Definitely a ride by, but it's gonna take two of us. One to pedal and one to jump and swing. Are you in?"

"I was never out."

"Atta boy," I nodded.

"Well, I know what part I'll be playing," said Perry.

"Was it ever a question?"

"Both of them or one?" Perry asked.

A smirk prefaced my answer. "We'll wait until they split up to get to their cars. I'll go for the taller one's knees first," I said. "He'll probably hit the ground, scream for help. I'll take out his other knee so he can't walk. Ride toward the other like you're gonna run him over. Delay him. I'll pay the same favor to him. Once they're both down, I'll go for their ribs. Ride back around. I'll mount up, and we'll head home. Too bad it's not Fatty and Skinny."

"Stay away from their heads," Perry said.

"Why?"

"If you crush their skulls, they won't remember a fucking thing."

"Yeah. I want them to remember. Good idea."

It was the best-laid plan—until I shared it with Naomi, who talked me out of it.

*****

When Naomi instructed me to meet her at the foot of the Algiers Ferry ramp during our first meeting of our second summer, I wondered how we'd put my bike in the Montego. When she arrived in a new, red FIAT, bike rack included, I imagined how we'd do "it" in a car no bigger than a condom box. I imagined her letting me drive in and out of St. Charles Avenue traffic—the only road devoid of a road marker running down its center.

I cut my driving teeth using a stick shift before I had a license. Big Moe, our Vietnam Vet neighbor, had thrown me and Perry the keys to his VW Beetle. We'd take turns spinning donuts and fishtailing Madison Street shells until the motor 'bout croaked. Driving, along with cigarettes, beer and church wine, and sex with my married teacher were life's pleasures I had experienced before I was halfway through high school. Crime and drugs remained off the list. So far.

"How do you like it?" she asked.

"Looks fast, but I never heard of FIAT."

"Stands for Fix It All the Time," she said. Her grin depicted more giddiness than concern. "And it has four on the floor. We can cover the lakefront, City and Audubon Parks, and bike at all three."

"Or two," I said. I hoisted my bike behind hers, ready to ride.

"Or one." She slid her hand across my waist while we slipped away to our seats. The new car aroma brought back memories of the day I first got in the Montego. The same day I purposely missed the school bus to play the good Samaritan.

"Make that four places," she said.

"Four?"

"My house." She zipped the FIAT through the Quarter and up Elysian Fields.

Naomi was ready to spread her wings. The confined space of the Montego candy bar car had run its course and elevated the heat of her frustration. I was just a kid happy to be at the candy store. Our second summer was Christmas in July gifting the perfect gift—7333 Ligustrum. Using her bed was something I was never going to suggest; the possibility of Val walking in proposed too great a risk. But I discovered that Mrs. Cat wanted to play while Mr. Mouse was away, FIAT in the driveway, and no neighborhood cars nearby.

More out of curiosity than jealousy, I did ponder if Val and Naomi were still "gettin' it on." Naomi never said. And I never asked. I didn't want my curiosity to kill the drive of Mrs. Cat. In my sordid mind, I surmised they were not, given she was seeing me at every turn of the screw. And if they were, was she seeing my smiling face from start to finish? Some things were better left unasked and much better left unanswered.

Lunchtime had arrived the same time we did, which to my stomach meant PB and J, but she had another meal planned. I had stood in the kitchen waiting for the bread to be spread when she escorted me to the edge of the bed spread, the size of four front seats. Naomi locked the door and closed the curtains across the back-door sliding glass. Blackness blanketed the room. My pounding heart blanketed my chest.

She walked and parked between my knees and rested her arms on my shoulders. I no longer waited for invitations and opened her short-sleeved blouse—looking ahead to what I had seen in the past. "The clip is in the back," she said.

She wanted me to work, and I aimed to please. My face pressed to her stomach, and I explored, placing kisses around her navel while brushing her hips. She cocked my head and massaged my neck. When she could stand no more, she pushed me flat and climbed.

"Do you love me?" I asked. Her hair scraped my face, the way it did during our first embrace.

"I do."

"Truly love me?"

"I truly love you," she said.

"Will you stay with me even after I die?"

"I will always love you, and I will never leave you." I wanted to own the certainty of the moment and all those to come, to assuage any doubt and that she would stay with me no matter the circumstances.

Naomi whispered the joy of finally being in a bed, then placed her tongue to the back of my mouth. I slid her summer shorts past her hips and encouraged her downward progress. My heart raced as she bathed my inner thighs and unzipped my shorts. My hands caressed her shoulders until she ascended, and we joined as one. Her hips rocked with relentless fervor.

Naomi dismounted and moved to her back, taking me with her. I returned favor and buried my face south of her tan line. She groaned and grasped my hands and embedded her nails into my skin. I separated and slid my hand beneath her hips. She rolled until I pulled her to all fours, her backside in front of me. We stayed until sweat soaked and secretion stained the sheets and sobbed until our souls were satisfied.

CHAPTER 14

Forget the FIAT. My adolescent biker goal had become to take the Lakefront Ligustrum trek alone, devoid of supervision. Although an ulterior motive existed, I was simply trying to adhere to what aunts, uncles, and parents alike had demanded: go outside and stay outside until it was time to eat. With the exception of the teacher, life in the summer of '73 was no different than many prior. My brothers and I were free to roam with my mother's knowledge of our whereabouts.

But the time had come to cut the apron strings, to ride off my mom's radar and complete the fifty-mile round trip against the odds and elements. Sixteen and nothing but rock and road under my wheels—a step closer to unadulterated independence. Going solo provided another means for Naomi and me to meet, and we created and embraced all options. I was determined to find or make a way. Everything seemed possible knowing Naomi was the catalyst who spun my spokes. I was saddled and ready to ride.

"No way in hell you're going across the river by yourself!" my mother screamed. I was strapping my transistor radio to the handlebars, when her ever emphatic voice had broken over the airwaves. She was wearing a housecoat and pointing a spatula, the long part of her arm. I fell from riding a high to an emotional flat tire.

"Yes, I am going!" I said. I was equally as emphatic.

"No, you are not. I know where you are going. You're going to see *that teacher!*" My bones shook, and my mind shifted gears up and down, thinking of names and ways word got out. But I was going to take one step closer to manhood or cower down and pretend Naomi was nonexistent.

"Yes. I am going to see *that teacher*, but others will be there, too."

"What other people? Who and where are they?" she asked. I thought the better of speaking my mind. *Who said "others" were people? I'm talking about her dog, McKeaver.* Nor did I reveal the times I had crossed the river alone, *that teacher* waiting on the other side of my everything.

"Guys from the bike club."

"You're lying! You're going to meet *that woman*. You'll regret it. So, get off that goddamn bike!" *That teacher* had been downgraded to *that woman*. I didn't take kindly to either. My mother's voice characterized Naomi as a bitch, a whore or worse.

"You and what army are going to stop me? None! Nobody!" She grabbed and tugged the handlebars, until I pulled with greater force. Tears ran down her face. Determination ran up my mind.

"I'll call your dad!" she screamed.

"Go ahead. I'll be at the lake by the time he eats lunch!"

As I dashed to catch the ferry, the battle raged. Her words penetrated my thick skull which was at war with my soft heart. Maybe it was the shock of her knowing about me and *that teacher*, but more significantly, what was I going to regret? After all, what could be better than spending time with a lady who was older, smart, and beautiful? The questions hit home.

Though I was certain my mom knew none of the intimate details when she slammed the spatula to the ground, perhaps she was referring to her own experiences. Those from her father and my dad. But the fact she never spoke of her past did nothing for me in the present. She beat my head with a crucifix and a religion I had already capitulated. Instead of advising based upon her own trials, she held up a rosary from behind a stained-glass window.

With an alcoholic father, a husband who drank, her struggle with depression and raising six children in a shoebox, years later I came to realize my mother did the best she could. And I believe she wanted what was best for her child. But I was too stubborn and too much of a self-centered teenager to have listened. Or I was too hooked on the passion and promises of *my teacher, my woman*. Love and skin were a powerful thing—more powerful than history.

The heat and humidity were unforgiving. And I loved both. The hotter, the better. The faster the temperature rose, the faster I pushed my three speed. The stretch of Elysian Fields lay before me, dressed in trucks and trains moving about their day.

I stopped to adjust the radio. The roads of New Orleans had shifted the dial set from WTIX, an AM station I had listened to since second grade. My fondest memories resided at Mel Ott Pool. I'd take a song underwater then pick up the lyrics when I surfaced. The songs were saturated into my psyche, I had listened to enough brokenhearted love tunes to suggest they were describing my future.

I hopped back on my ride and captured a clear signal of a song, which ventured back six years, imploring a lover to let his conscience be his guide. It left me wondering if I were just Naomi's toy, a plaything which satisfied a hidden desire. My mother's voice played along in my head. I shook off the static and searched for a convenient store.

*****

In New Orleans, Dixie Beer was slightly second to the deity root beer—my favorite to wash away po'boys, fried pies, and hot afternoons. I grabbed a long neck and downed it upright. The only thing wetter was me, leaning against a store wall, dripping from head to high white socks. Naomi's front door was an hour out, and I deviated from a path she had shown from her new, red car. Forget the FIAT, I again reminded myself.

Pontchartrain Beach Amusement Park had risen from the lake where Elysian Fields ended. Naomi's bike club apparition greeted me at the front gate. I pedaled east, parallel to the Zephyr—a three-hill, wooden roller coaster monster. Her ghost and my mom's noise grew louder with the clickety-clacking chain pulling cars to its zenith.

Would I go to hell? Who the hell told my mom? Would I get kicked out of school? Would the teacher get fired? What would Val do? Does she really love me? What will I regret? Is this the beginning or is it the end? The questions repeated at the speed of the descending coaster, muffled only by screams from riders who fell like hell to their possible demise. Turmoil ruled, until an automobile horn had blown me back to the shoulder of the road.

Two minutes later, the lake came into full view, wearing the sun's face which had opened its eyes to a tranquil, morning horizon. The breeze and salt water pressed into my pores. I dug deep on the climb of the Seabrook Bridge, then coasted into the backside of Ligustrum Drive, little squares of grass trimmed to perfection, every other house a duplicate.

"Well, you made it. I was a little worried," Naomi said.

"Yep, me and my transistor radio. It's amazing how clearly I could hear the songs," I said.

"It took you longer than I thought."

"I stopped to get a beer, and the chain came off the track." She cocked her head, puzzled. "A root beer," I said. A grin stained with soda crossed my face.

"And you're sweaty!"

"And stink like a teenager should."

"Would you like to take a shower?"

"I guess. I've never taken a shower. Closest I've come was running through the Mel Ott Pool sprinklers, and that water was always too cold. I'd love to feel warmth on me, but I'd hate to get back in these clothes."

"I'll wash and dry them. I'll find a pair of shorts and a shirt for you."

"Why Scarlett, you're such the lady," I said. Clark Gable parted my voice.

"Why thank you, Rhett. I think you know your way to the bathroom." Scarlett parted hers.

125

Naomi placed her hand on the knob and turned. Steam clouded the room, and I stupidly stepped into scalded water. Warmth cascaded my '70s' hair on the second try, reminding me of the breeze which had blown against me an hour ago.

"Are you okay in there?" she asked.

"I love it!" I pictured Hawaiian waterfalls, mermaids, and dark-skinned ladies wearing hula skirts wishing to lei me.

"Really?"

"Yes, ma'am. I'm only used to…" Naomi slipped behind me, wearing only a smile.

"I thought you might need some help," she said. Naomi wasted no time lathering me while she rested her head between my shoulders. Water trickled between us. Her hips, hands, and breasts gyrated, until my legs had gone weak.

"Val shorts?" I asked. My body was cleaner, but the thought of wearing his shorts dirtied my mind.

"No, a pair of my brother's old ones. And a T-shirt, too."

We made our way to the living room, ate chips, and drank iced tea; "Saturday in the Park" played in the background. We danced while we sat, toes laughing, shoulders hugging, elbows and knees rubbing. "Let's take a ride. I want to show you something," she said.

Our shower and my borrowed clothes were knitted to my skin when Naomi had gassed the FIAT toward the lake. She parked the car at the foot of the levee, as though we were in Algiers. We were greeted at the top by a pier and a white house, both which appeared larger and made impregnable by the blue sky.

"Is this a long walk off a short pier or a short walk on a long pier?" I asked.

"Neither, funny boy. Let's sit on the levee. I wanted you to see this. One day, I want a house with a boardwalk where we can hold hands, read books, and take naps while listening to the ocean."

"California or am I just dreaming?" I asked.

"Yes, California. You and me. I promise," she said.

"By then, I'll be able to drive. Will you ride down Ventura Highway with me?"

"Up and down, all day 'n night long," she smiled. "And we can watch the sun sink into the sea."

"You really promise? Your word is more important than breathing."

"I promise. I'll get a teaching job, while you pursue acting. We're gonna go."

"I know. I believe in you. From the start, I've believed every word you've said." Joy bolted through my veins, and hope and anticipation filled my eyes. The words of regret my mom had spoken had evaporated. Naomi had spoken California, homerun promises, locked in a vault of heavens. Acting was my one and only occupational dream, and she was my one and only ticket into the movies.

"Will you use your name or a stage name?"

"I was thinking stage. James or Jimmy McCarthy. It sounds a little like McCagney."

"Your middle and my maiden! Clever!" An adult and a younger pelican passed over. We watched them disappear into humidity.

"Maybe one day, I can become a writer, if acting doesn't work out," I said. She placed her head on my shoulder. Her hair sheathed my face. I smelled the soap and shampoo she used to cleanse us. And to put smiles on our faces. Sitting on the levee and trusting her promise had become the defining image and moment, which suppressed any reservations of her love and commitment. "But first, I have to get out of these clothes."

*****

"Please be careful," Naomi said. "I'll see you in a few days." Thunderstorms brewed in the distance. They had grown closer by the rumble. Humidity had worked its magic. "Think of me!"

"All the time!" I said. I waved good-bye and watched her walk back inside.

Despite the evening traffic, I returned on her shorter route. A deluge welcomed me at the foot of the Chef Menteur Pass. Gravel churned and covered my teeth and sunglasses, a much cheaper pair than Coach Jennings had sported. The tires sunk into the grated drawbridge, and I struggled to maintain a grip more challenging than the one my mom imposed. Cars sped inches from my face, and Naomi's shower knob had more life than my dead legs.

Soaked, hungry, and exhausted, I reached the five o'clock ferry. Watching the boat workers was of little interest. I longed to be back at the Ligustrum Lodge, taking on hot water and Naomi's hotter body. The thought took my mind miles away from what might be awaiting at home.

The rear starboard stern stayed meshed to the dock as the boat pushed away. A figure flashed from the ramp, sprinting toward the boat. *He'll never make it...please wait...don't...*His right hand landed on the ferry rail. His knees cleared the height, while his left hand held a lunchbox above his head.

Had my dad been in the Olympics, the judges would have scored him a ten in the pommel horse event. He walked toward me, then detoured to the upper deck. Something must have blinded him. My heart which pounded was all I could see, save for the cross atop St. Louis Cathedral. I wondered if my mom had called him. I blew it off. I was too filled with the day, too filled with Naomi, and too filled with what tomorrow might bring.

CHAPTER 15

Our second summer together had come and gone far faster than we wanted. It had flown at the speed of heat lightning following an evening thunderstorm—laughter and love at every turn, burning the bed with gluttony, complete with up-and-down moments. Some were too close for comfort.

The day my dad had cleared the ferry railing and thereafter, he never said a word about the teacher and me. And I never offered, until the evening twenty-five years after I had met with Naomi at Joey K's. Maybe my dad's past prevented him from approaching me.

My mom remained mum, also. Perhaps her past was too painful to regurgitate. She either accepted the situation or I had become better at hiding my tracks. It helped, also, that I had friends to act as alibis, so Naomi and I could return to our Saturday routine as my junior year began, even as football sailed through the air. My world had evolved away from sports and revolved around her and a future in which love had provided.

The new school year presented a heavier workload for her. She occasionally appeared disconnected, stating she had less time for letters or to drive me home. A handful of eyes greeted me with stares when I boarded the school bus. Less letters and less rides made for an unpleasant student.

I dusted off any notion of apathy and despair and instead chalked it up to her occupational obligation. Cause for alarm was put to bed after blissful Saturdays in the park. And I still held the image of her head on my shoulder and the ultimate in my ear—her promise, during our time at the pier.

By November, skies had turned gray, day after day, giving the bikes an early winter respite. Christmas called, marking the near end of the semester with three remaining when I'd receive my graduation gift—California with Naomi. I listed *12 Angry Men* and *A Streetcar Named Desire* on my acting resume—productions limited to the library. They gave me confidence, igniting a light in my future with her. Which could not be said of her disposition in the FIAT that day, which blended insipidly with Saturday's clouds.

"There's the Prytania Cinema," I said. Months prior, she had taken me to the Gentilly Orleans Cinema to see her favorite flick, *Butterflies Are Free.* We sat in the corner of the last row, holding hands and sipping soda from the same straw. I longed for her to take me to the Prytania, New Orleans's oldest operating theater.

"Yep," she said. We remained silent, as the FIAT headed toward uptown.

We sat next to a tree on Ring Road in Audubon Park, the smaller but more historic than City Park. Audubon bordered the river and St. Charles Avenue pulchritude and was split by Magazine Street. It offered a diversion of activities on both sides—the zoo, golf, picnics, walking, jogging, and biking. Audubon also served as an oasis for Loyola and Tulane coeds wishing to study or light a fire under the elderly oaks.

"Remember how Ray C. and Stevie P. left for the lake without us on the first bike club trip? I thought you were going to blow a gasket."

"Yes, I do." Egrets waded in a lagoon. A man sitting on a bench at the edge of the water was wrapped in a coat and a book.

"Can you hear it?" I asked.

"Hear what?"

"You have to put your ear to the ground," I said. "When I was a child, I'd place a penny and my ear on the railroad track, estimating when the next train would come along—as though I could determine things to come from miles away."

"Really?" she asked.

"Yep. I can hear hundreds of family feet running and racing down Monkey Hill right now. Huge picnic. Tons of cousins. Bon Temps at da Audubon." Naomi looked skyward, as though she had used her eyes to determine something far away. "Are you okay?" I asked.

"Huh?"

"Are you okay?"

"Yes, go on."

"Like I was saying, good times. I first learned to swim at the Whitney Young Pool. My 'old man' dad helped. Eventually, the zoo seals became my swim muse. And I loved the train ride. Naomi? Mrs. Wagenbach? Are you sure you're okay? It seems like I'm doing all the talking."

"Somewhat," she answered. Naomi displayed the Debbie detached face, which had remained with me over the years.

"You're unusually mellow but not unusually beautiful," I said. I thought a compliment might change her mood.

"I was thinking we could go for a streetcar ride. We can catch one in front of the college," she said. The mention of streetcars stirred memories of acting, Saint's football games and a Super Bowl David and I attended. The St. Charles rail ride was a breathtaking alternative to the Claiborne Avenue route our family had taken in the station wagon, heading to Tulane Stadium.

"This is how I sat in our Rambler. Always seeing what everyone else saw first," I said. I had folded one of the two streetcar seats forward like those in the funeral limos.

Naomi faced downtown, while I watched uptown fade away. I took in what St. Charles Avenue had given—a heaven of majestic mansions, opulent palaces, and Southern Oaks. The streetcar swayed to a wedding waltz. I envisioned ghosts on a wrap-around porch, while Crepe Jazzmen blew their musical scent to shadows and warm spaces. Naomi and I embraced in our reception dance, as hors d'oeuvres and highballs flew among the apparitions.

The opened windows permitted a cross breeze. I lifted my collar to get my best Bogart look, then stepped out of character to practice a touch of Brando—making an offer to the riders they couldn't refuse. "We can't go on like this," Naomi said.

"Would you rather I sit beside you?" I asked. The smell of beignets blew by when we crossed Napoleon Avenue.

"No. That's not what I mean," she said. "We have to end this." She reloaded her bow. The arrow pierced my Adam's apple; its tip had stuck in my throat, spewing poison. I could not force it down, and I struggled not to vomit.

"End what?"

"Our relationship. We can't do this anymore." I stayed silent, letting eternity pass. My eyes burned to the back of her head. A banging had pulsated against my temple—keeping time with the discordant streetcar—as though it rolled over a penny with each excruciating beat.

"I don't understand. '*We*' *have to* end this? '*We*' *can't do* this anymore? Because there is no *me* in that '*we*'," I said.

"I have to end this. I think we should just be friends," she said. Seven words more final than death.

"What? Why?"

No answer.

"Perhaps you didn't hear me. Why? Tell me fucking why!"

No answer.

I was left to hang, like the Mardi Gras beads wrapped to the streetcar electrical lines. A hundred thousand volts jolted my veins. My mind raced to keep pace with my heart.

"I don't understand! What about the promises you made about California? The letters you wrote?" I asked.

"Not so loud," Naomi pleaded.

"Oh! That's why you're telling me on a streetcar, thinking I'd sit quietly. I don't care who hears this, Naomi Blanche DuBois! Was I just your little high school toy? You could take me out to play then fuck me whenever you liked?"

"And I can't go to California with you," she added.

"No California, and you just want to be friends? That's it? No explanation?"

"Yes." In less than a mile, I felt decimated and dirty and discarded. At that moment, I thought my life had ended.

"Are you shitting me? Over two years have gone by and you got out of bed and decided today was the day to end our relationship? No forewarning? Not the slightest hint? And you promised you'd love me until eternity was through? You fuckin' lied!" I realized I was saying everything to her saying nothing.

"Please lower your voice," she said. She looked around to see who was looking around, caught in a prison of her own device. Being embarrassed was more important than the hurt she had heaped upon me.

Anger swelled inside me. Rage sat on a razor blade, cutting my intestines into pain I could never measure. I lost my ability to reason. I wanted to punch the windows and walls and anything or anyone who drew close. Cars and houses flashed in a strobe light. Blinding tears drowned in my emotions. My hand shook as I reached and shook the streetcar chord.

"What are you doing?" Where...going? Come..." The iron wheels and the clanging of the bell disappeared downtown. Her words fell faint and feeble and vanished into the ashen firmament.

CHAPTER 16

While Naomi lived in freedom at Shaw, I remained in perpetual pain and in an inexplicable fog. The river was the only place in which to turn. It was where I spent Saturdays saturated in numbness, watching boats go by and contemplating a list of those whom I could or should seek.

Go to admin or a counselor? I couldn't trust them, and that would have incriminated both of us. They might fire her, though this appealed to my psychosis.

Talk with fellow students and friends? They would have awarded me a medal of accomplishment, while jealously claiming how they wished they had been in my shoes. After all, a boy should have been quite proud of such a feat. Accolades and sarcasm would have come from every corner of campus: *Hail King Richard the Lion Hard-On! Nixon's got nothing on you Tricky Dick ll. Naomi, Naomi you tickled her fancy and got in her panties! How's the weather down there? How are the twin peaks up there?* On and on, it would have gone. And I would have laughed had I found it funny.

Speak with my parents? I would have been better off in Vietnam.

Go to a priest? My suspicion of the shady side of man-made religion had come to fruition when I discovered that I had company. Brother D, Shaw's Mr. Do "it" all, had handpicked my younger brother to help with a job in the pool storage room, specifically to place a chlorine box upon a shelf. Bro. D offered to assist. He placed his left hand on my brother's chest and his right on the boy's crotch, squeezed both, then thrusted his hips and rod into the rear of the freshman's pants. My brother remained still and silent—a lamb who'd been led to slaughter. Skeletons remained in the pool equipment room, while Bro. D danced at the Bourbon Pub and Parade Disco during the night. He weaved and bobbed around the school during the day, until he found an opening.

Drink wine? It was off the table after my cousin and I had been kicked out of the altar boys. The balcony organist was not amused when she saw us fall flat to the rear altar floor—pretending to be asleep during one of the 6:15 a.m. mundane masses.

Beer? No longer an option after the fair fiasco. Never a bar bottle nor cup had graced my lips during my time with Naomi. She had been the beer, the bottle, and the bar satisfying three spirits within—me, myself, and I.

I had become a walking dead boy in the city that care forgot. My eyes never adjusted to the darkness. So, I blindly searched some more. And in many of the wrong people and places.

*****

"Bra. It looks like the blues got a hold of your shoes," my neighbor Gary said. "You're home early. Did the bus drop you off?"

"Yes, to both," I said.

"Come on over when you can. Perry and I will be upstairs." Gary lived with two siblings and parents who smoked more than Slim. The downstairs was occupied by his aunt and his eccentric, semi-handicapped cousin who rarely saw the light of day and whose skin resembled the light of day.

"I'll try," I said. I crossed the street, bookless, no longer caring about what was taught or who taught it; for all I cared, Archbishop Shaw could have gone up in smoke—napalmed—the way I was when I had stepped from the streetcar.

"What's happening, bra?" Gary asked. He sat cross-legged, picking his guitar and wearing a handkerchief around his head. Perry sat on a couch, wearing a grin and squinting through his glasses.

"Nothin', man," I said. "Been down. Way down. And I don't see a way up."

"He needs some medicine," Perry said.

"Wanna smoke some hash?" Gary asked.

"Hash? Like hash potatoes?" I asked.

"Not quite, bra," Gary grinned. "Hash is a solid form of grass." He no longer spoke to me like the kid he'd known prior to his enlistment. Time away mellowed him. He returned from Germany with a few vices military men learned during Vietnam times.

"Grass?"

I had heard through the grapevine, news reports, and watching Woodstock footage that people were taking trips without leaving their houses. Outside of alcohol, I had no firsthand experience of what was sending folks on moon voyages, while their rocket ship stayed planted to the ground. I had been too busy living on Naomi's "love drug."

"Grass is the street name for marijuana. Mary Jane. Pot. Weed. It comes in different names and different ways." I stood listening and thinking how I was getting an education at another high school.

"Why do you smoke it?" I asked.

"To get you fuckin' high, bra. Chase dem blues away. Put your mind at ease, on a trip from what's bothering you. I learned about hash overseas. And it's easy to score some here in the states." The lingo Gary used was foreign to me, but I did understand that he would have to have a hell of a lot of hash for me to forget the pain I was experiencing.

"Is it like beer?" It dawned on me why older folks were calling younger folks "potheads," while the same older folks stumbled in a stupor from beer, wine, and whiskey.

"Better than beer, bra," Gary said. "This shit makes you laid-back. None of that crazy ass, screaming shit people do when they're drunk." That explained his personality change. And I liked it. "Come on. We gotta go to the back porch."

"Is this stuff illegal?" I asked.

"Damn, Herzy. Stop being a killjoy. People drank alcohol when it was illegal."

"Well, that's the truth. Some people still do."

Gary placed a squared, brown block into a bowl attached to a metal pipe no longer than my middle finger. We were perched above the neighborhood; the river snaked in the distance. A boat sailed by Perry's Wharf, reminding me of the levee times Naomi and I rocked the Montego. And how, at school, we had been reduced to two ships passing in the middle of the day.

Gary lit the hash and took several puffs, then handed it to Perry who expanded his chest with one inhale. My turn. They stared at me with conviction and snickered at my drags.

"Damn, Herzy! Don't be afraid of it! Drag that shit!" Gary said.

"Like inhaling a cigarette?" I asked. Smoking had taught me something, since David and I almost died when my mother made us smoke in a room the size of the FIAT.

"Dat's what I'm talking about! Inhale and hold it for as long as you can. Then slowly exhale," Gary said.

I complied and waited for the big, bad buzz they described. And waited. Ten minutes went by when the surroundings shifted. Peace and laughter enveloped me—a Gulf of Mexico calm on a storm-free sunrise. My mind drifted easily through the Big New Orleans. Time stood still—the way it did when a boy fell into his true love's embrace. Until the sun set.

My feet never touched the concrete toward home, and my mind never touched Naomi. Maybe I had found something which could take her lands away. "Breakfast for dinner, Mom? You have any hash browns with those eggs and pancakes?" I asked.

"Do you see any hash browns?" she asked. My siblings sat at the table, arguing about who would get what. I thought how they could use a little hash. Mother included.

"Slow down, Bobby. David. I mean Mary. Tommy. I mean Richard," my mom stammered.

"May I have some more?" I asked.

"There is no more. Be thankful for what you got."

And I was. Especially after hearing an evening news anchor deliver the daily Vietnam casualty report. "What a waste," my dad said. He stood shaking his head. Perhaps he was thinking of his war, the lost souls, and those currently dying from living with the consequences of trying to stop the spread of communism.

At least that's what we were told—words, like hash, were blowing smoke up the citizen's psyche. "The world's gone to pot, Pop. Gone to pot."

*****

I had officially become a member of the higher society, a daily blast into space from Gary's launch pad. My vacations to Mars were inevitably met with a return trip, while leaving a piece of my brain behind. Each time I journeyed upward, I spiraled downward. The low was as low as the high was high, a crash and burn which compounded my depression, which increased my disdain to be at Shaw.

The first two weeks of the second semester of my third year were miserably damp, wet, and cold, even though I had lost the Naomi rain in my life. I sought solace against a home wall heater, where I again begged God to take me in the middle of the night. He politely declined, which left me no appetite to face Naomi nor to catch the school bus. Most mornings, I didn't. I stood on the corner of Franklin and Americus and waited for the city transit, which dropped me four blocks from the school's front doors.

The disciplinarian was irate; my parents were equally as caustic. My heart smiled knowing I had missed homeroom plus the first two classes. Threats of suspension and this and that discharged from the three of them. I considered their consideration, then missed more school bus rides and became acquainted with the city driver. He encouraged me to get to school on time, or I'd one day be driving the public masses for a few pennies a day. I genuinely considered *his* advice after I received my first three-day holiday, compliments of Mr. B.

By the time the suspension ended, I had advanced to smoking real grass from real paper, modeling Uncle Wille who had rolled his cigarettes. "Smoky Mary" was no longer a stretch of road from the

Quarter to the lakefront. On day one back in prison, fate would have it that I'd meet my new smoking partner in the Shaw hallway.

"Hey, man. I saw your car. Nice wheels. How did you get it?" I asked La Tib. He and I had been St. Anthony classmates since kindergarten. We had history—large family, altar boys, baseball and football, McDonoghville kids who took crap off nobody.

"I've been working at La Ruth's and saved some dough," he said. "But it's in my dad's name." La Ruth's was an upscale restaurant located one block from where I caught the city bus. It was a Berdou's competitor and paid more money. The thought of applying there never crossed my mind; George and idea Ida had my loyalty.

"Nice, bro. I don't make enough at Berdou's to own a car." Save for papers and pot, I owned nothing but depression and the lack of will and a way to snap out of it—too blue to realize that the same money I was spending on pot could have been placed aside for a vehicle. "But I do have something that can make you fly, a little Smoky Mary. I've been having trouble getting to school on time, and I can make the morning load lighter, if you give me a ride. I'll roll if you'll roll," I said.

"If you'll buy, I'll fly." He smiled the smile he had in our football huddle, a fire plug offensive lineman who'd fight at the drop of a helmet. I suspected he'd give me the jersey off his back had I asked. I also had a hunch our home lives were two trains on the same track. We asked no questions. We were more interested in wearing an illegitimate smile than wearing one turned upside down.

"I guarantee we'll both fly! We'll put the *high* in high school!" He had a big laugh for such a succinct guy.

*****

La Tib arrived on time in his '72 Camaro. He had worn his mind and tie loosely, and so did I. My mother was pleased that I had risen to the sound of her command, swallowed some cereal and combed my hair, but inevitably commented how I needed it cut.

The Camaro boomed to the beat of an eight-track stereo. I encouraged my new chauffer to take his time—I had a manly man joint the size of a Cuban cigar, rolled right and tight with a crisp dollar bill, a slow burner ready to blow. At each stoplight, I placed the lit end in my mouth, sealed it with my lips, leaned over, and fired a shotgun, which damn near choked La Tib to death. He pulled the car to the side of the school entrance gates and did the same for me.

My first two period teachers were glad to see me, sarcastically stating they thought I had withdrawn from school. Even the disciplinarian acknowledged my punctuality. They all complimented my artificial, Rio Grande-size smile. And it was just as dirt muddy.

The buzz lasted until I crashed at the end of third period. I was hit with an insatiable hunger which was appeased by my lunchtime hamburger habit—a side mound of fries smothered in ketchup and a dollop of mayo. Both kept me feeling fat and fine.

"Well, Mr. Herzog. I see you're eating well today, and that fly of yours is down," said Father LaDuca. He had graced the cafeteria with his presence.

"Oh, thank you. I thought you might be hungry," I said.

I had taken a seat next to La Tib, letting it be known that he had serious lunch 'n' munch competition. We devoured our food and would have licked the plate had LaDuca not been standing at the end of the table, shaking his head. I emptied my trash and headed to class, thinking how learning with or without Naomi was the same, but each resided at the opposite ends of the curve—oblivious during my Naomi natural high times and Mrs. Demeanor days; oblivious during the dark days.

Algebra 2 was the worst subject taught by the worst teacher during the worst time of day. At the start of the semester, I had decided to take my first and only "F" and recover the credit in summer school. I also decided to go comatose in less than a minute after my bloated butt hit the desk. My math instructor, whom I had dubbed Mr. Math Monotone, was okay with my siestas, since I caused no trouble, and

I didn't snore. Each day, he greeted me with "good night," which I acknowledged with a sleepy nod. Except that day. There to welcome me was Mr. B, school disciplinarian.

"Mr. Herzog, Father LaDuca would like to see you in his office," he said.

"Why? What did I do?"

"That's something you need to discuss with him." I was upset that I had missed my nap, but LaDuca was livid.

"How dare you insinuate that I'd perform some perverted act, simply because your fly was down! It's the most repulsive thing I've ever been told! If your parents, whom I have contacted, were not such devout Roman Catholics, and if Father Gerrard, whom I've also contacted, were not a friend and your parish priest, I would expel you from this school!"

"I…"

"Shut up! Do not say a word. I am suspending you for three days for your vulgar comment and for your vulgar mind. I hope you go to confession and pray that God the Father Almighty forgives you! Now, get out!"

"I…I don't understand."

"I said, 'Get out!'"

LaDuca's voice rang in my ears; water welled in my eyes. For the second time in three months, somebody had ambushed me. His verbal ass whipping was more than I could or would take, returning me to the time when the little league coach had son-of-a-bitched me. I had offered a priest food from my overloaded lunch plate, and he gave me three days off with no chance to explain.

As I walked to my locker to place books in and take nothing out, I swore to never again take another whipping of any kind. I may have been too young to go to Viet-damn-nam, but I was ready to enter my own war.

I waited against a drink machine outside the cafeteria crime scene, anticipating the ride home. I would have preferred riding the city bus, a funeral limo, or with La Tib. My mom's eyes shot lasers from her glasses, as the car came to a stop. I rolled the window down as we exited the gate and shot a big bird—the size of a Cuban cigar.

*****

Three days on our Americus Street provided plenty to ponder—was exacting punishment and pain worth the price? Be it on my mother, father, pseudo priest fathers, nuns, teachers, coaches, or bullies—the line was long and so were the consequences for a moment of temporary pleasure.

I never considered myself to be violent, but the tendency to seek justice grew over time after the beatings by my parents, the dog mauling, watching bullies maul helpless kids, drum set thrown away, trophies discarded and the worst, Naomi, whom I ironically thought would make all the pain disappear. Instead, she had broken my spirit and my desire to live.

Three days of isolation and maniacal planning were equally filled with unanswered questions since LaDuca told me to "shut up." Did he know about us and was he sending me a message, hoping I'd transfer to West Jeff? Was she pressured to end our relationship to avoid the fallout? Did my mom go to LaDuca after my solo ride to Naomi's house? Questions ran through my brain at the speed of a runaway train, engineered by LaDuca, conducted by Naomi. I laid tied to the track.

All these questions and no answers meant one thing—go see Gary. While the parents were away, I got high each day and looked ahead to more rides with La Tib. But on day one of my return to Shaw, I decided to catch the city bus, so I could inform the driver about what happened, and I could not resist the pleasure of being late following the suspension.

"Are you kidding me? A blow what?" the driver asked.

"No, sir. I'm not kidding. He insinuated I wanted *him* to give *me* a blow job, when I just showed him I had enough food, if he wanted some." The driver laughed so hard he passed the next stop, and a lady holding brown-papered, grocery bags stacked to her eyeballs.

"Man, that's dead wrong, cat. Try to stay out of trouble," he said.

I walked the four blocks to the school entrance, wondering what lay on the horizon—thirty degrees with wind gusting off the river, trying to light a joint I had stuffed in my sock, nothing but matches in my pockets.

CHAPTER 17

Saturdays once spent with Naomi and sitting on the river wearing angst and my marijuana masks were now spent with an original love—baseball. It had been an integral part of my childhood, and an ember still burned in the pit of my heart. I thought it would provide a mental escape from her, and it helped when a fellow classmate encouraged me to give the sport another try now that the third football season had passed by.

B. Southpaw had given me the name Bozo the spring of my junior year. He said I looked like a clown with my cap pressed down over my wiry hair. BS, the name I had given him in curt response, was one of the few people whom I had hung around, especially after his dad died, crushed by a load of pipes which rolled from a flatbed truck. He had a hunch why I had given up playing sports after ninth grade, but he never peppered me with questions. But not everyone was as meek as B. Southpaw.

"Zog, tell us about it," Owie said. Coach KY had called for him and Ro to warm up their throwing arms. I voluntarily trailed them down the right field line.

"Tell you about what?" I asked.

"Come on, man. You never tell me shit. How did you get with Naomi?"

"How, or Owie has to know?" I asked.

"What did you have going on? As in 'Me and Mrs. Jones,'" he said.

144

"One of my favorite songs, bro," I threw back. For a moment, I had felt like a kid again—the glove and baseball in my hands, the smell of grass, bubble gum blowing, bursting sugar across my face.

"Back off, Owie. It's nobody's business," Ro said. Owie and Ro were KY's heralded freshman who, like the rest of us, were headed to another school because of a condom box. Naomi once said he stood inches from her hip, pressing for answers and for a closer look at her cleavage. All six-foot-four of him. KY had the build of a milk bottle baseball bat with catcher's legs and an average throwing arm. He was slow as a sloth and had lumbered around campus carrying a caustic disposition.

"He's just smilin' in my face, Ro," I said.

"Okay. You ever been to her house?" Owie continued.

"A few times."

"What's a few?"

"A few several."

"How did you get there?" he asked. I didn't mind the verbal game. Word play was my methodic response to such questions, and I held the cards. And I decided when to show them.

"She'd pick me up or I'd ride my bike. I remember one time, *the only* time, I had to ask somebody for a ride. I was desperate." I flashed back to *the only* night visit to the Naomi pad, a strange night I did my best to describe:

> We rode in Billy's Blue Baby, a Chevy with a 350 engine and a standard transmission. Regular cab. Fast out of the hole. Billy pushed hard to New Orleans East. He had a cigarette in one hand and the steering wheel gripped by the other. An ice chest stocked with beer ponies was in the truck bed, trying to stay cool amid the summer air.
>
> "Thanks for taking me. I won't ask again, but I have to see her," I said.
>
> "You have to go squank," Perry said, elbowing my ribs. He sat in the middle, smoking one of Billy's cigarettes. I sat with my head out of the

window and my big feet on the floorboard, trying to avoid the smoke and motion sickness. I did what Naomi taught me during our carousel moment—focus on one thing…I chose the point of convergence where our skin became one and my mind had been set free.

"We be makin' love, child. She done declared it," I said.

"Call it what you want, bra," Perry said. "You're gettin' one hundred percent USDA prime." I elbowed his ribs. We both chuckled.

Billy parked on the Ligustrum curb and grabbed the brew. Naomi placed a bowl of chips on the coffee table, told them to make themselves at home, and gave them free fridge access. She marched me to the bedroom and made me feel at home and gave me free access.

She wasted no time stripping, and in a heartbeat covered me, skin to skin, my mind extricated into ecstasy. Convergence. We made time stand still but not the clock, when a soft knock landed on the door.

"How much longer y'all gonna be?" Billy asked. Ninety minutes had flown by, along with the chips and beer. Perry laughed in the background and requested more of both.

"Not much longer," I said. "Just a few more minutes."

Naomi rolled me over and knocked my knees at the rhythm of a woodpecker and sent me flying to a perpetual pleasure island, fast out of the hole, faster than a 350 engine.

Nobody asked where Val was, and Naomi never said. She just kissed me good-bye.

My head rested against the truck tailgate. My hair blew in the smoke free wind. I watched the city lights dance in the distance from atop the industrial bridge apex, as we motored toward the Vieux Carre.

Billy and Perry walked and watched naked women dance on Bourbon Street bars; some swung out of windows while sitting on trapeze seats. I stayed in the truck bed, thinking of Naomi's bed, counting stars as luminous as her smile. Neither light show cost me a dime.

"Man, I wish I could have been in your shoes," Owie said.

"I wish I could be in your cleats. At least you're getting to play today," I said. "I can't prove it. But Coach KY hates me for some reason. Probably the teacher thing. And y'all heard what he said on the bus. He called me an idiot and accused me of blurting out the 'N' word to that car."

"Don't let him bother you, Zog. He hates most students. Still, you're the luckiest guy in the world. The big cheese on campus," Ro said.

"Besides," Owie said. "You shouted back that it wasn't you."

"Sorry, Ro bro, but I don't feel that way, and yes, I shouted, but truly guys, I was buried in Naomi thoughts."

"Big cheese," Ro reiterated.

Big cheese caught in a big mouse trap was more appropriate. I wondered how highly they may have thought of me had I been the adult sleeping with a female student. Would they think a difference existed between the two? Were the scales heavily tilted against an older man? In an environment in which I was taught to sweep suspicion under the rug, how or where would I go to seek help? Boys were told to take the pain; suffering produces character. But my character kept wishing and hoping she'd return.

"Time to take the field, Bozo!" B. Southpaw said, knocking my cap off as he sprinted by. Coach KY announced the starting lineup in the dugout. I took a seat on the bench and watched the game.

*****

Monday's practice was lifeless, a hangover under a cloudless sky. A dropped fly ball in the final inning of Saturday's defeat provided another excuse for Coach KY's nefarious mood.

"Herzog! Get your glove and go to centerfield. I want everybody to see how a fly ball is *supposed* to be caught!" he barked.

"Watch out, Bozo!" BS said.

Fly ball number one remained in the atmosphere, falling between second base and shortstop. I sprinted and turned my back to the sun. The ball landed in the web of my glove.

Fly ball number two chipped off the bat barrel, lobbing a Texas League blooper over first base and into foul territory.

Number three skyrocketed near the stars I had counted from the truck bed in the French Quarter. My capless hair covered my eyes as the ball hung for an eternity against the blue backdrop and hid its stitches on the face of the sun—until it chipped the tip of the web and shattered my nose.

"Somebody. Go get a towel and take him to the office," a voice said. Blood soiled the grass under me. I saw a bat resting on black coaches' shoe.

CHAPTER 18

"I have an ulcer."

"An ulcer?" Mr. B asked.

"That's what the doctor said. I've been having a hard time eating and sleeping. Can't even put down a burger and a full plate of fries." I was late for PE, leaning against a post, staring at room 111. I was in a trance trying to figure out how I was to endure my remaining time at Shaw while knowing who and what caused the ulcer.

"What are you worried about? A guy your age shouldn't have a worry in the world," he said. "You're only in high school. Wait 'til you're my age, then you'll have plenty to worry about." He sounded like my mother who sounded like my father who sounded like everyone older—a broken record playing a clueless song. "Whatchya have? Another year left? You need to play football. It'll take your mind off what's worrying you, guy."

"Yep, only in high school and another year left." After a two-year affair with my married English teacher, I didn't think I'd live to be his age, nor was I sure I wanted to. More importantly, I had traded my love for football for the love of Naomi, and I didn't see how one year of playing could cure my trials and tribulations. And evidently, Mr. B had yet to hear about the baseball broken nose, or like others at Shaw, he chose to ignore it. "And who said I was worried about anything?" I asked. The only part of worry was woe, and I was doing my damnedest not to feel sorry for myself.

"Oh. Well, guy…watch that hair length. It's getting long. Get to class." Silence ensued. The way it did after a casket slid into a tomb, when folks mulled and looked at the sky for answers. He walked toward the cafeteria, worrying about terminally grave matters, like hair. I walked to the gym thinking, *Where there is no will, there is no worry.*

I had become ambivalent about physical education. I loved the exercise, but I detested the feeling of dizziness and puking, both undoubtedly Mary Jane induced. I welcomed the end of the torture, which meant the beginning of lunch. The fusion of pot and exercise was offset by the newly ulcered, half-portioned burger and fries combo—which left me a little less fatter and a little less finer. I stayed on the lookout for "Father Fly," sparing him the zipper search trouble, while I made sure my train was on its track.

The algebra nap continued, until I awakened to the part of school which had pushed me to the finish line—drafting class. Along with a cousin, a cat I called Weed Hopper, and Brian, the class was the one bright spot of the day. They pulled me out of myself, often reminding me of a true treasure—music. We spoke more about music than we did about drawing and girls, which was an appreciative hiatus. Music was our NOLA blood. Big and easy.

"Man, you gotta go see the Z! Their sound blows the top off your head," Brian said. He had curly hair, longer than the rules allowed and a mellow disposition for a guy who played the intense game of football. His older brother was a Shaw assistant coach, and they were north and south opposites.

"Where have you seen them perform?" I asked.

"First time I saw them was at Pontchartrain Beach. And they played for free! People were going apeshit! You walk away thinking, 'How can three guys with three instruments put out that much power?' Next time they're in town, go see 'em. I promise, man, you'll never regret it." I was dubious about the "promise" word, but not about his excitement. Had my math teacher instructed with his kind of energy, I would have stayed awake long enough to pull a D.

"Where else have you seen this band?" I asked.

"At the Ware…"

"Herzog and company! Please work a little more and talk a little less," Mr. V said. He was T square straight but a rare teacher who let us talk while we worked. If we worked.

*****

High school summer number three and my first without Naomi approached. The anticipation was agonizing. Seeing her around campus was equally tortuous. She laughed, frolicked, and flirted with the faculty and students and acted like I was invisible, as though nothing had happened. It forced me deeper into isolation. My moods worsened from angry to angrier to angriest. And having to ride the school bus fueled the fire.

"What's up, Zog?" a former St. Anthony classmate asked. Like La Tib, we grew up together since age five. By high school, he had been branded the name "Turtle," because his face morphed into a snapper. Unlike La Tib and me, he watched us practice football from his steps during the Green Team's undefeated run. It wasn't that Turtle was too slow, it was because his skin color kept him out of the park. Deb peeking from one end of the fence and him from the other, both looking outside-in with wishes in their blue hearts.

"Just headin' home, bro. Not many days until summer hits," I said. As I plopped onto the window side seat in front of them, a caustic disposition had inched up and down my spine. I had seen Naomi leave with the same faculty teacher she had arrived with on two consecutive mornings. I contemplated approaching him and to offer a meticulous description on where and how she desired to be touched, her favorite positions, and what made her orgasm. Mostly, I just wanted to stomp his ass for being next to her.

"I heard that, Zog," Turtle said. He had sat on the last bus row accompanied by a basketball player who carried a chip on his shoulder. Both had been talking louder than I could tolerate.

"Hey, bro. Will you please move your elbow out of my back?" I asked. No response. I politely asked a second time and received the same response. "Hey, bitch! For the third time, get your fucking elbow out of my back, or I'm gonna break off in your ass!"

"Who you callin' bitch?" yelled the basketball boy. He jumped from his seat, both fists clenched.

I jumped just as fast and slid my head to the left, as his right hand landed squarely on the metal window support. I countered with a jab to his throat, then blocked his roundhouse. The lack of space left me too pinned to punch. I grabbed his shirt and leaned in, when other students stopped us.

The bus and the vehicles behind us came to a halt on the Westbank Expressway. Horns howled, and birds bigger than my Cuban cigar had flown left and right. The driver got busy informing us that he would inform the office; I got busy informing the basketball player that we could go again, as soon as we exited the bus.

"If you fight anymore, I'll do everything I can to get you suspended," the driver said. "So, make sure you go separate ways. I'll be watching. And *you*, come up front near me." I almost son-of-bitched him from my new seat and wanted to fight him, too. But, I could nil afford another suspension. The hot water I had been in that semester just got hotter.

Basketball boy and I received the opportunity to find alternative transportation to and from school for the final two weeks. La Tib saved me in the morning. He kindly wanted to go kick Turtle's ass for not doing something as simple as moving his arm. I encouraged him. When Naomi heard the news, she unexpectedly stopped me in the hallway, acting concerned.

"What is going on?" she asked.

"What's going on? What do you mean?"

"Someone told me you were kicked off the bus for fighting."

"It was a skirmish. If he had the balls, he would have picked it up after we got off the bus, like I asked him," I said.

"What *is* the matter? What *has* gotten into you?" Every time you see me, daggers come out of your eyes, like you want to fight me."

"*What's* the matter? *What's* gotten into me? Why ask the obvious? Are *you* fucking clueless? *You* are the matter! *You* are what's gotten into me! I got into a skirmish because of *you*! I don't sleep or eat because of *you*! I have a fucking ulcer because of *you*! Have *you* no fucking shame? How do *you* stand here and ask these things?"

"Please lower your voice and stop cussing," she said.

"Fuck you, and the streetcar you rode on, Naomi! You sound and look just like you did that day."

"Please call me Mrs. Wagenbach when we are at school."

"*I'll* call *you* what I want. Bitch would be good for starters," I said.

"Okay, okay. I'll tell you what. I'll drive you home for the rest of the semester," she said.

"Oh, a charity ride? Is this your feeble way of apologizing? What are you going to tell the boys you've been riding with? Or would *you* prefer *me* to tell them?"

"Look, let me at least help you with this."

I had to accept, and I hated it. La Tib was not an option. He had to hurry home and get dressed for La Ruth's. Waiting on my mom, whom I never told what had happened on the bus, would have expanded my school day two hours. I was trapped into receiving help from the person I loved and hated the most.

The hot water had reached a boiling point, but unlike her, I admitted my shame—hash, weed, bus skirmish, suspensions, Algebra F, no football, Catholic albatross, no Saturdays with Naomi, no Naomi summer—the list was almost as long as the cast I saw on basketball boy's broken hand.

That and metal window supports gave me a crooked smile.

I should have walked or hitchhiked home. Either would have been better, knowing the two-week taxi ride would do nothing to help me mentally. Naomi made small talk, and over the course of nine days, I replied in smaller yes and no answers. It was all superficial sounds signifying nothing. She was applying a band-aid on an incision deeper and wider than the deepest and widest canyon.

"Why?" I asked on day ten.

"Why what?"

"Why did you end it?"

"I...I don't know. I guess I thought it was best if we were just friends," she said.

"You guess? So, you're uncertain? And how does that happen? How do you go from supposedly being madly in love and planning to go to California to just wanting to be friends? How can a forever love become so temporary, and now the temporary love feels like forever?" Naomi stared toward the river from the VFW parking lot, one of our many former drop spots. A garbage container wreaked of whiskey. Save for glancing at her watch, she was motionless. "Will I see you this summer?"

"No, I can't."

"Why not?" I asked.

"I'll be taking graduate classes at UNO."

"Really? You have time for classes, but no time left for me? It's summer! We were all about summer!"

"Why are you getting upset? Please calm down."

"I figure it's the only way I can get you to answer these thousand unanswered questions which are haunting me! You can't see me, or you don't want to see me?"

No reply.

"How do *you* think *you* would feel if I had been the male teacher and *you* had been the teenage girl student?" I asked.

Nothing.

The scene sounded streetcar similar. Same script. Same silence. I opened and slammed the FIAT door hard enough to rattle her teeth. My shoe met the fender with the force of a sixty-three-yard field goal and created chasm the size of a canyon, a dent the size of the one in my heart.

I hoped she had a good explanation for Val. If not, I did.

*****

The time had come. Summer school. The most paradoxical phrase in my New Orleans vocabulary. The ultimate oxymoron; and I was the ultimate moron whose summer fate had been declared on the first day of the second semester during year three, when I capitulated to the lowest common denominator. But when I discovered who was to join me on this academic adventure, it didn't seem as badly as I had imagined.

"Don't Bogart the joint, Humphrey," I said. Grit hung the paper bud from his lip, sucking the life out of it.

"Yeah, yeah, yeah," he said. Grit steered his Cadillac jammed with tunes and high school delinquents—Shades, Perry, La Tib, Hog, and myself. Our attitude, not our aptitude, had landed us in the predicament, a cast riding uphill against a Catholic wind, which confused and compounded our misery. "I'm trying to smoke this summer school shit out my mind. Math! Who da figured?"

"I'm paying the price for sleeping during Algebra two, too," I said. "But Mr. M makes math understandable. This cat can teach. He wears his pants too high, but he can teach. I even find it interesting, the fact that I must go through a process to get an answer. The guy I had after lunch during the spring could have cured the worst case of insomnia, but I should have put forth more effort."

"The difference between now and then is that we can go in with a nice buzz," Grit, my fellow flunky, said. We were bad in math, but we were great with numbers—smoking a couple on the way. Along with a Black Molly, the goods helped push us through class after a late night in the Cosmos—a French Quarter bar which never carded us.

"And I can learn with a smile on my face. And I'm makin' a frickin' A!" I said.

"Fuckin' A!" Grit replied.

"We gotta give Grit's wheels a name," Shades said. He had the personality of a rug—laid-back, and he wanted to attend Shaw as much as I wanted to miss a summer with Naomi. "How about Benny and the Joints?"

"The Brown Bomb," La Tib said. He honored Grit's brown caddy, since his brown Camaro had been sidelined by his dad.

"It looks like a bomb exploded with the amount of smoke in here," I said. "How about Cheek and Bong and the CarPool Fools?"

"Muff diver," Perry said.

"Muff diver?" I asked. "Like you have any muff diving experience, and it damn sure isn't 100 percent USDA, if you have." Perry elbowed my ribs.

"Oh, like you have any, Zog," Hog said. Hog reminded me of a young Louis Armstrong. His face carried a wide smile and whiter teeth than my picture partner E. White.

"Ah, I don't know about the Zogster," Gritt chimed in.

"He's right, Grit. I'm a virgin," I said. Everyone fell silent. It was the sound of Naomi never answering my questions.

Grit slid the caddy in the teacher's old Montego parking spot. We went forth to redeem ourselves.

*****

The time had come. Summer school was done. Several months removed from the breakup and soon to become a high school senior, I reestablished my relationship with my buddy the beer. Too many nights in Cosmos helped, too. I also forged a stronger grip with Miss Mary Jane and occasionally drowned in a Quaalude quagmire, while stealing Valium from Maw-Maw's medicine cabinet.

I trusted the chemicals could take me to a place Naomi once did. The highs were blissfully insane, but I became trapped in a prison of pot, pills, alcohol, and Shaw. The baseball experience had been far less than I had hoped for, and school was a wasteland—a salmon run, upstream swimming against a current of white shirts and ties. The medicinal buzz kept me alive, but I didn't want to live anymore. Living in misery had to be worse than being dead. Even with a summer school "A," I was slipping back into darkness.

Many were the mornings when I barely knew my name. Broken heart, broken nose, broken. Many were the mornings when waking up for school was the second hardest thing, since sex had exited Naomi's backdoor. Many were the nights when I spent lying with my face to the wall, thinking, *No Naomi. No sports. No future. No idea what college was and no will to find out. Parents. Beatings. Church. Getting high. School. Someone somewhere had it worse, but I didn't care. Nothing but a large amount of nothing. Dead boy walking. The time had come. I've crossed the bridge ten thousand miles, since I saw him leap. My turn. Plan it. No audience. No popsicles. No rescue. Let death win. Climb the catwalk on the bridge and commit to the nightfall; disappear into the black water which dares me.*

*****

In New Orleans, and possibly throughout the south, the most desirable place for a band to perform during the seventies was the Warehouse. And for three reasons—its setting, its sound, and its spirit. Located on Tchoupitoulas Street, the nineteenth century bricked building had originally been used for coffee and cotton storage.

The facade had two elephantine doors to allow passage for wagons, oversized loads, and an overflow of exiting concertgoers. More difficult and dangerous was entering through a narrow, splintered door. The single entrance resulted in a pushing, shoving, general admission crowd vying for front row dibs. Bourbon Street on Ash Wednesday smelled better than we did after we handed over our five-dollar tickets that August night.

The guts and backbone of the makeshift concert hall were "bricks, wood, and good," which provided an impeccable acoustical miracle. Lumber rafters supported the walls and ceilings. Some schizo souls sometimes climbed and perched on a crossbeam, their feet hanging above the stage. I never understood the fascination, especially knowing a person could get higher and never leave the rancid, carpet-covered floor.

I stood with several of my new friends, elbow to elbow. Concerted freedom. A rushing wave of peace painted with a common purpose. Sweat had poured from every piece of our skin; a ceiling fan or two worked overtime. The lights went down, and the screams and matches went up. Dark and dank, the pot flowed with the river a hundred feet behind the stoned walls.

Three wise men had ridden from Texas and took the stage. Beer drinkers wearing boots, blue jeans, and a couple of cowboy hats. One mustache. One beard. One free from facial hair. Two guitars and a simple drummer's kit. When he wasn't slithering and sliding the neck of his Les Paul, the lead man placed his ten-gallon Stetson on the tip of a larger-than-life steer horn attached to one of a dozen Marshall amps.

The raw, blistering blues freight train tone had taken a three-hour journey, downtown center of my head. It kept rockin', and I stayed on board. I was exhausted and floored by the epiphany. And I found a new lease on life. One week prior, I had chosen that night to jump. But I had harkened back to Brian's words during drafting class. "Man, you gotta go see the Z!" David, Perry, Shades, Billy, Ray, and I had to cross my suicide bridge to get to the show. And nobody was going to stop the vehicle, so I could take a run and leap into eternity.

The Warehouse and music prevailed. I found hope and a new influence, a desire to be alive in the world. It was as though Jesus himself had left Chicago simply to save me.

But the ecstasy of seeing the Z was briefly neutralized by the memory of my drum set. The show was a reminder of what I *might* have been, but not what I could have been, had my drum dream not been tossed to the street. *Might* would have given me the chance to have been on the stage or to at least pursue the possibility. After the high school debacle, I had given serious consideration to take lessons on my own dime and time, but I was too paralyzed by the pain. Too late to pick up the pieces. Instead, I had to learn how to love reality— to come to terms with knowing Perry and I found our band, but we were never going to be in one.

While my childhood brain had burned before it had been developed, and while Naomi had emotionally emasculated me, I was determined that no part of her was going to kill me. It was a matter of death and life. That night at the Warehouse stayed with me every day. Still does. The ulcer had subsided. I planned to live until eternity was through.

Three Wise Men

Part 3

CHAPTER 19

"Puking blood, huh?" my dad asked. His voice showed no concern. Although I had planned to live forever and beyond, a disconnect existed between the *want* and *how* to. Old vices were hard to break, and some had grown careless and detrimental.

Three years out of high school, I continued to flounder, still lived with my parents, and had not a clue what I wanted "to do or be" in life—except to stay stoned, chase ladies, drink, and dance. And not always in that order. I was failing at trying to forget the Mrs., while searching for a surrogate.

"Yes, I started vomiting blood when I was running," I said. I had been in the middle of a self-prescribed hangover cure—jog in cotton sweats until the fifth of straight rum had purged from my system. I bought into the cultural mind-set that age twenty-one was to be the big, birthday blowout, which made no sense since eighteen was the legal Louisiana drinking age at the time.

"What do you want me to do?" my dad asked.

"Call an ambulance!" I said. He stood behind me, showing no sense of urgency. I continued to flush bile down the commode.

"I guess I can drive you to the hospital," he said. *I guess*, translated, meant "no money" for an ambulance.

The constant stop and go of the Chevy wagon nearly splattered whatever remained in me against the window. I bargained with God—let me live and I'll never touch another drop of liquor; beer, maybe, but not liquor. In the distance, an emergency light screamed my name. And I was listening.

Joe E was the chief meter reader for the gas company, the place where I settled after I acquired and quit more jobs than I could count. He, like many of the company "lifers" who bitched and complained about their job, went home, and drank beer and bitched and complained some more. The "lifer's" angst became pearl words of wisdom, which worked wonders, especially after I turned twenty-one.

"What did the doctor's say?" Joe E asked. He stood at the foot of my hospital bed. Sans a dress and heels, he was a replica of Corporal Klinger on *Mash*—same height, nose, and hairy body.

"Gastroenteritis caused by alcohol poisoning," I said. "Hey, Joe E, y 'all reading in the Avondale area?"

"No. Why?"

"There's a sweet little thang I want to visit again. I saw her sunbathing when I walked to the rear. Told her, 'Just here to read your meter, ma'am.' She invited me back a few times to reread it. If you know what I mean?"

"Shit, Richie. You gotta get it together and get out of this meter reading crap. Make something of yourself. Stop screwing around. You want to wake up ten, twenty, or thirty years from now and be stuck like us? Go to college. You're too smart for this." Joe E preached this sermon several times, mostly to help people like me and Perry who had joined our motley crew three months after I started.

"I must look like a genius lying in a hospital bed. And college? Hell, I'm still trying to get out of high school."

"What are you talking about? You've been out of high school for three years," he said.

Three years. I was the most miserably joyful student to have walked across the stage that May day—grabbing the diploma and crying the tears of a clown. And like many of my confused classmates, the world awaited me. College never registered. The thought of more school made me want to puke blood. Or enter a psych facility. Reading meters was blue-collar work for this blue-collar boy.

"I got a diploma, Joe, but I never graduated."

He knew nothing about Naomi. I was free from Shaw but imprisoned by her memory. I wanted to tell him all of it—her. Hash. Pot parties. Many a ménage à trois. Tuesday's two sisters who lived across my street. Medicinal Russian roulette. It was a vicious cycle—feel better to feel worse to feel better again.

"I don't know which you had more of, Richie, jobs or women," Joe E said.

"I only know the jobs have lasted longer. Maybe the partying and screwing around are just superficial ways of dealing with things that have happened."

"Life doesn't get any easier. And we damn sure don't get any younger."

He left, but his words remained. I was starting to listen to his blue-collar advice. Another voice joined Joe E's, telling me I was wasting my talent. It was the same voice which convinced me to return the condom box. Both voices lent me options—lay in bed while feeling sorry for myself or get up and do something about it.

After sunset, I faced a window and stared at the orange and black sky. I squinted beyond the dirt and recalled the promise I had made to God, then made a declaration—I was going to become a football coach. Perhaps it would protect boys from the Naomi-type teachers. Perhaps it would help ease my pain.

At the end of day five, I was released from the hospital with no work or play restrictions. I took a walk to the river with David, Perry, and Gary. We stood on the train bridge connecting the levee to Perry's Wharf. The sun reflected radiant ripples off the river—the same sun which had burned me, when I had flown headfirst to its surface. The man whose legs had hung from the bridge replayed in my mind. I remembered how I had planned to do the same, when three wise men saved me that august night at the Warehouse.

"You lost a lot of weight, bra," Gary said.

"Yep. Trying to look like you. 'Bout died, though. I never knew drinking a straight bottle of rum could poison me. But I gotta tell ya, it sent a powerful message."

"I told you about drinking that shit, Herzy. That's why I smoke da pot."

Perry and David dropped boulders over the railing. I felt at peace watching the splashes coming close to hitting us thirty feet above. Gary lit a joint and blew the smoke into dusk. He stretched his long, skinny arm toward me, the paper pinched between his thumb and index finger. I passed.

*****

"Why don't you come to Ole Miss?" John F asked. He was my fast-running, faster-talking neighbor who had become the most highly recruited quarterback to play at Shaw. As kids, we played touch and tackle football in his front yard. Although he was four years younger, in a camera flash, he surpassed me in pounds and inches. "You can try out as a walk-on player. I'll talk to a couple of the Ole Miss coaches."

Amid the myriad of meters being read, I attended Shaw football games to face what had been taken away. I had to walk through the fire surrounded by fanatics, the band, the distaste of Shaw, and memories of the teacher to feel the shame and the pain. Cheers and music filled the exits after victories. I exited the meanest, maddest person determined to one day coach football. But unlike my Warehouse *might-have-been* moment, where my drum set had been discarded and where lessons were required to pursue playing and forming a band, I now endured something far more challenging and distressing—the *could*-have done.

Sports, specifically baseball and football, came to me naturally. The only prerequisites for playing were practice time and diligence—two requirements an athlete embraces because he or she loves the games, not because it's work. Naomi's weaving web and luring offer to spend time together brought me to the acute realization and regret that I had been robbed of sports during the most essential time of my life. More excruciating was the reality that I *could* have done what I saw being performed from my stadium seat. The train had passed me by, but I used it as motivation; I had to find a new one running down similar, athletic tracks.

"What's Ole Miss like?" I asked. My only recollection was watching a guy named Archie "Who" beat Arkansas in the 1970 Sugar Bowl. David and I sat in the North End Zone, as the star quarterback raised the MVP trophy. Flags waved in the chilly wind.

"Beautiful and bootyfull. Girls galore. But Oxford's a different world, nothing like New Orleans." Besides athletics, our common bonds were females and a desire to uphold a liquid diet. To hear him describe it, Ole Miss was an oasis of healthy, wealthy, Delta ladies looking for love, and the town seemed to have the exact number of bars in which to find them. College quarterbacks had magnetism, and those girls brought friends along.

"I've never heard of Oxford. Where is it?" I asked.

"North Mississippi. Near Memphis."

Memphis I had heard of because of our commonality—the blues. But Ole Miss could have been near China, which was not far enough. I was scratching an itch, a Naomi rash which said run as fast as you can. Divorce New Orleans or die young. A change of scenery was indispensable; new memories and footprints were calling.

"You know, I grew up LSU purple and gold, but I know too many people at that crazy-ass place. Too many temptations. I'd drown in a drink in Red Stick. I need to get to a school where I can focus and become a coach. I'm already five years behind my graduating class."

"Well, there ain't much to do in Oxford. You'll have plenty of time to study," John F said.

"Man, I haven't studied anything since high school, and I did very little of it when I was there."

"I'm talking about studying women," he said.

I laughed and let go of the thought.

*****

A year had passed since I had held rum to my lips. I had limited myself to two beers an outing and committed to lifting weights. Albeit I knew I would be a long shot, I gained twenty pounds and decided to not only visit Ole Miss but also to give football another chance as a walk-on player. The added strength would help considerably, too, if I had to battle players as big as John F and Stevie D, a River Ridge recruit who had driven us on my first Ole Miss visit in his Cadillac.

We rode passed endless, sporadically inhabited countryside. A plethora of pines and magnolias shouldered the interstate and backroads before I saw a Lafayette County sign, a pronunciation which bore no resemblance to our Louisiana City. We arrived from the west on Highway 6. From a distance, a water tower sprouted from the ground and the town came into view, a sanctuary sheltered in rolling hills covered in Kudzu and red clay.

"Next to that tower is the athletic dorm. You can see the top of it through the trees," John F said. As we drew closer, the tower and the dorm grew inversely proportional.

"This is where y'all will live?" I asked.

"Yep."

"Not too shabby." It was the first time I had seen a dorm exclusively for athletes. It sat like Mt. Olympus on the campus's highest point. John F tried to describe it in hyperbolic terms when he returned from his recruiting trip, but words could not depict its stateliness.

"We have the largest walk-on turnout in the nation this year, Richard, 127. That's a lot of kids, and to be honest, our scholarship players will get the majority of looks and snaps. But we'd love to have you, especially if you came up with John F," Coach L said.

He was the first college coach I had met, and he looked and sounded like Val, Naomi's first husband. Coach L had a lull in handing out room assignments and keys to football players, when he spoke to me. It was beyond comprehension how anyone could or would oversee a three-story facility housing over four hundred athletes.

"Well, I believe it's too late for me to get into school. I'm here to watch practice and see the campus, if that's okay. I probably won't come until January," I said. Too late meant I had no idea how to get into college but a greater knowledge that I could not afford it.

"Sure! How long are you planning to stay?"

"Just a few days. I'm on vacation and have to get back to work."

"What do you do?" he asked.

"I work for the Gas Company, and I'm about to be promoted to the service department. Blue-collar day for blue-collar pay. I'll install, turn on, turn off meters, light water heaters. Things like that."

"Folks will love you around Christmastime, if they can't pay their bill," he said. I felt like Scrooge, thinking if people couldn't pay their gas bill, they couldn't get anything for Christmas either. But I let it slide, since I had no intention of being employed come the New Year. "How you gittin' home?"

"Train or bus. I left my car at home," I said. Green with envy, I looked at John and Stevie. My curiosity stayed on the sideline, knowing damn well I'd have to sell my vehicle to pay for college, knowing damn well I *could* have had a free education, too—had I not punted football for Naomi.

John F led me down the second floor, carpeted hallway to his room—two beds, two desks, a sliding door closet, and a thermostat. Most impressive was the adjoining suite bathroom. Four football players shared two sinks, a shower, and a commode with toilet paper delivery—which had to be in high demand since the downstairs cafeteria was three times the size of my Madison Street house. When they were not busy cleaning their rooms, study hall, and academic counselor's offices, the custodial crew got busy shining the lobby furnished with billiard tables, trophies, and a color TV.

No sooner had I dubbed the dorm *Hilton on the Hill*, an underground explosion erupted—loud enough to push the Hilton from the hill. No sooner had we jumped when Big Chuck let himself into the room. Chuck was a mountainous man with a boyish face who swallowed up the light, a grizzly standing on hind legs. He was topped with red hair to match an agitated bear's temperament.

"What's up, Cajun?" Big Chuck asked.

"Hey! What's up, Chuck, think you could've knocked a little louder?" John F asked. I stood in the middle of two dense voices, which rattled the walls, as though Chuck and John were a hundred yards apart.

"Just ready to get on the field and bust some butt, bro!"

"Chuck, this is Bud, my neighbor from Gretna. Chuck's our center, Bud," John F said. He used the moniker I had been given from requesting barroom beer in a voice which matched theirs.

"What's up, Bud?"

I shook his island size paw, then politely excused myself. Discovery had taken the better hold of me, pointing me toward campus and perhaps to catch a glimpse of the summer school ladies. Laughter filled my shoes, as I walked down a steep hill, picturing quarterback John F with his hands between center Chuck's Harvey Canal wide cheeks.

I landed at the Union Bookstore walled with miniature mailboxes and every Ole Miss athletic apparel a fan desired. A framed inscription outside the upstairs restroom caught my eye. And my soul. "The University gives a diploma…but one never graduates from Ole Miss."

The words I had spoken to Joe from the hospital bed reverberated. It took hours for me to absorb the coincidence. I walked it into dusk, then straight into Churches, a holy dive off the Oxford Square. The structure bore a bricked, Warehouse resemblance. A host of students and early fall arrivals anxious for football parties to begin had lined the walls. Tanned coeds were lost in trance conversations with athletes who were lost in wishful thinking of getting lucky. Except for Big Chuck. He was howling and belting lyrics, begging to spoon under a full moon with a love he had lost.

"Pascagoula boys," John F said. We both shook our heads. I had once asked Naomi if that was where she borrowed the *goula* word she spoke, wrote, and exercised on me. She duly informed me that *goula* was "butt" in Italian.

Big Chuck let out another howl, and another. I was certain no bar bouncer had the vulva to escort him from the premises. Near midnight, a cry arose from a far corner, as though they had answered Big Chuck's mating call.

"What was that?" I asked John F. "What are they chanting?"

"Oh! You gotta hear this cheer. They say it over and over at football games or when a bar's about to close. Craziest cheer I've ever heard!"

"The bar closes at midnight?" I asked.

"This is Oxford, Bud. When we're just getting cranked up back home, this town is shuttin' down," he said. I wondered why John never went to LSU. I never asked.

"Maybe folks should start drinking earlier," I said. "Lot of nice girls, though. Maybe they should change campus to campussy." John F laughed until tears fell in his beer. I sulked in stupidity—shamed for losing control of my tongue, seeing women as objects, while trying to fit into the aura of the moment.

In the time it takes to shuck an oyster, "Are you ready?" begged from an opposite corner until Churches joined in Sunday morning unison:

> *"Hell yeah! Damn right!*
> *Hotty Toddy, Gosh a'mighty*
> *Who in the hell are we? Hey!*
> *Flim flam! Bim bam!*
> *Ole Miss by damn!"*

I was uncertain what my future fellow students were chanting. But the rally cry offered a relevant question: *Are you ready?*

CHAPTER 20

Being ready and being able resided at opposite ends of the earth. It resembled my Pollyanna "plan to live forever" moment exiting the Warehouse. And once again, I was clueless on how to accomplish where I needed to go. Entering college presented some tall hurdles, which required every day, every minute focus. And perhaps most importantly, I had to train myself how to stay calm amid the impending storms.

The aspirations of acting and athletic participation were behind me, and I was determined to look forward and to focus on coaching football. Coaching is what drove me. My occupational passion had now become the pigskin. But equally as powerful were the remnants of Naomi's skin. The first step of change was to get out of my environment. Oxford was the only change. Challenge one, of step one, stared me down one Saturday morning in a classroom at West Jefferson High School.

The school, which had been branded "the place from hell," was conducting standardized ACT testing. The reality was simple—score high enough and you are admitted to Ole Miss. Don't and you won't—keep your meter reader pencil sharpened. And I was under no illusion that the university would spread its doors open, because of what I experienced in high school.

I felt like I had entered another universe, younger fellow test takers were dressed for church. Eyes gawked at me, the old man, dressed in faded blue jeans and a NORML shirt—a pot plant emblazoned front center wreaking of cigarette smoke. I had worn it the night prior to Jed's Bar, where Muddy Water's played the blues until

3:00 a.m. During intermission, I watched David and Mr. Muddy shoot billiards. "Ain't that a man," I hollered each time he sank a ball. Right then and there, I knew I had some Mississippi in me, more than the water which flowed a few blocks away.

Right there and then during the test, I revived the blues which had washed over me a few hours earlier, trying to answer Math, Science, English, and History taught since Socrates. My head hurt and so did my pride, knowing I knew little and there was much to know. Sadly, my education had been reduced to a car seat, a bedroom, and a blanket at The University of Naomi.

My ability to correctly answer problems sunk with the cue ball with the eight still on the table. I had created a system based on the instructor's advice who stated, "Guessing gives you a better chance than leaving a question unanswered." I guessed until my pencil turned blue, too, enough that a pattern of figures formed, leaving me hopeful that a machine somewhere had an identical template—one which graded millions of ACT tests while making millions of dollars for a college whose endowment exceeded the national debt.

Six weeks later, I had discovered that my guessing was equal to my lack of knowledge and my lack of maturity, since I had spent the night before soaking suds while out howling Big Chuck. A letter congratulated me for participating and "bla, bla, bla," as I read each word about as carefully as an Algebra 2 equation—taking less time than it did for Mr. Water's cue ball to spray the others from their tight triangle. ACT score: 15.

The number seemed good, since I knew not what qualified as acceptable. I like the way fifteen sounded, and it had association—Audubon Park Golf Course hole fifteen; my age when Naomi first straddled me in her Montego. I imagined people slapping me on the back, toasting the score with an expensive bottle of Sangria. Until my admission's letter lassoed me into reality.

Dear Mr. Herzog,

Thank you for your admission request to the University of Mississippi. We are sorry to inform you that your ACT score did not meet our minimum requirement of 18. We encourage you to either retake the test or petition to enter. If the petition is granted, you will be placed on academic probation for your first full year. During your probationary period, you must maintain a 2.0 GPA.

We wish you the best in your decision and in your future endeavors,

Sincerely,
The Office of Admissions and Records

The letter was a ballbuster, reducing an already low self-esteem to its smallest depth. The ACT was a sad act in a play repeated with mistakes and forlorn encores. And I looked no further than the mirror—a reflection of no focus and preparation. But I also looked at fifteen as a number, one which, unlike summer school Algebra, measured my aptitude, not my new attitude. I looked at the score as a missed field goal, only three points away from the university's requirement. I was never to be satisfied to reach the minimum. I failed the test, but the test had failed me—not measuring the tangibles which can show up in a classroom.

To whom it may concern:

Thank you for your letter concerning my admission application and for the opportunity to petition. While I understand that my score was woefully short for admission, I can honestly state that a standardized test is in no way indicative of my work ethic and my desire to attend the University of Mississippi. I can also state with confidence that no number is large enough to measure my hunger, heart, and drive to one day receive my diploma from the University...

Writing reminded me of the frequent correspondence I had with Naomi. It was the second letter I had written since we had sworn eternal passion and promises to live and die on the California coast-line. My desire to enter Ole Miss was filled with the equal intensity of our relationship. But destiny was now driven by a single driver—me, no we. All I needed was a chance.

"Hell yeah! Damn right!" Four words had shaken my mother from the couch.

"What? What is it? Why are you screaming?" she asked. *We are glad...inform you...accepted...probationary...Spring semester 1979... We look forward...Ole Miss*...tears blurred the words, as I reread the letter, then erupted into that crazy cheer.

"I'm going to college! I'm going to be a football coach! I'm going to get a degree from the University of Mississippi! And I'm never gonna graduate from Ole Miss!"

After waiting several agonizing weeks, I covered the sad ACT score and rejection letter sitting on the kitchen table with the new news—sealed with the knowledge that I had to maintain a 2.0 grade point average to remain college eligible.

"That's great! But how you gonna pay for it?" Mom asked. Not since the last time I had pitched and won a game had she joined in my exuberance, proud of her son in spite of the rocky road we had traveled.

"I don't know, but I won't be asking you and Dad for a dime."

"Well, dat's good, 'cause we don't have it. But if we did, I damn sure give it to you. We'll help however we can."

"I'll find or make a way, Mom." Challenge number two was heavier than the books I had carried up Sue's steps when I was a kid but not as heavy as the baggage Naomi left me holding. I knew that if I could survive her and a hundred jobs, I had hope and I'd fight every step of the way. She was the big if.

*****

The tan, '76 Camaro banked two thousand out-of-state tuition dollars, a clean machine I had proudly purchased new. The car sold the same November day the ad appeared in the *Times Picayune Newspaper.* As the owner drove away, I thought of the million meters, barking and biting bitches, and the frigid and torrid temperatures I endured to save for a down payment. Enough to keep my monthly note at $127.

The new owner glanced in the rearview and waved good-bye. I laughed as I recalled the sexual escapades—the feels on wheels; how more smoke billowed from the windows than a Cheech and Chong movie; how I painted the dome light red to capture the local whorehouse mood; and when I drove La Tib to Thibodeaux for a Lynyrd Skynyrd concert, two free birds blowing joints on a special Saturday night. I wished the young lady well, safe travels, and a cleaner, future existence. I stood carless, knowing I'd have to depend on others for a ride.

The '76 Camaro banked two thousand out-of-state tuition dollars.

Two months after I bid adieu to the Gas Company and the Camaro, I sat in John's 280Z, gazing at the white wonder which blanketed the Ole Miss campus. Light reflected from the snow. The tires crunched the powder as the car crawled to a halt.

"That's the statue which is supposed to tip its hat, if ya gonna lose your virginity while you're here," John F said.

"That cat knows better than to tip his hat to us," I said.

A new home and future covered every inch of me, while a billion stars lit a path to the athletic dorm front doors. I unloaded my treasure trunk purchased from an army surplus store in Gretna. Naomi's letters, concert photos, and miniature steer horns were my prized possessions—worth millions in memories but probably not worth a dime at a garage sale.

The next morning, I hung the horns and pictures over my bed and placed my cowboy hat on the left side tip. I decided to make the ten gallon a part of my museum lore, reserved for fortunate eyes who graced our room. John said we should charge admission. One look at the memorabilia would certainly stimulate their curiosity, allowing me to part with my Warehouse wisdom.

Fifteen college hours and classes awaited me. Fifteen matched my momentous accomplishments—the ACT score and the end of my innocence. The number also infused timidity. Even on the brink of twenty-three, I felt intimidated by younger, smarter, wealthier Ole Miss preps dressed in starched khakis, loafers, and buttoned-down shirts. I dressed in flannel shirts, blue jeans, and white socks, sensing a thousand look-alikes looking at a stranger in a strange land.

"Excuse me? Can you give me directions to the Education Building?" I asked the nearest, prettiest coed who came along. Not a hair on her head waved in the winter wind.

"Ah, yes, sir," she said. I disregarded the "sir," as she proceeded to explain.

"Tell me, please. Why do so many people dress up just to go to class?"

"Oh, most people are Rushing, so they have to dress a certain way."

"They're in a hurry and have to dress up?"

"No, sir. They're Rushing for a fraternity or a sorority. They're trying out."

"Sounds interesting, young lady. Guess I'll just rush along to class." She smiled her southern smile and walked away. I walked to class, then to day one of football strength and conditioning.

*****

Soreness saturated every muscle in my body and did not recede until the end of spring practice. Coach L was right. Though I never owned a moment of fear, I received very few reps, and my skills had deteriorated significantly since ninth grade. So did my academic acumen. Though I managed to squeak by with a 2.1 GPA, my grades were equivalent to my aching bones. And my bank account was worse than both.

By semester's end, the two thousand Camaro dollars had evaporated. No money. No place to stay. No car. I was forced to return home—loaded with guilt that I had to rely on my parents. Though my uncle Clay lived with my Maw-Maw until the day she died, there was a stigma attached to older males who lived with their parents. Men were supposed to be independent and strong, the caretaker. The males I knew at my age were going forward. Twenty-three and little to show for it. The sad act had grown sadder.

"I wished I'd made more than two grand from the car sale, Mom." I said. She listened while she made my favorite potato salad. Summer number four since high school arrived, the fifth without Naomi. The taste of her skin and the potato salad remained stuck to my tongue. "I thought I could stretch the money, but out-of-state tuition and this fee and that fee and living expenses were too much." While it had taken me four years to get to college, it took one semester to realize that a school wanted my money.

"What are ya gonna to do?" she asked.

"Work and save. I can't afford to live on my own and save for school, and I want to return to Oxford, to Ole Miss. I have a sense of place there. It calls me to come back. I'll never get a degree from anyplace else. Just not happenin'. And when I get there, I'm going to work harder to raise my grades like my life depended on it. Too many C's. I can, and I will do better."

"Never say never. Besides, you don't own a car. John F was your only ride. He can't drive you to work." He was my main ride but not my only ride. I found, on occasion, hitchhiking to be a reliable source to get up and down I-55, but that was not revealed to my mom. "You know, we will let you stay here. If that's what you want to do, do it. I've always said you can do anything you want, if you put your mind to it," she said. Simple, sage, motherly advice.

"It's more than I want. It's what I need. My mind and my heart are on the same page for once. I'm bound and determined to make it back. Even if I have to hitchhike." The environment I desperately needed to escape had become the place where I was financially forced to stay. I had taken step number one, only to discover I landed two steps back. I was being tested—by a life never short of surprises, rejections, and climbing out of holes.

*****

Decent paying jobs were hard to find and returning to the Gas Company was not a consideration. My former meter readers would have thrown their route books at me. To make matters worse, the oil industry had gone in the tank. Inflation and interest rates had sky-rocketed. I took what I could find—from loading pipe onto flatbed trucks to cleaning public restrooms.

On my first job, I was employed by the dad of my best St. Anthony friend, Jay. On my first day, I watched cars standstill, bumper to bumper from the Gulf Station gas pumps on North Rampart to streets in the French Quarter. Gasoline had been in tall demand but short on supply, and cantankerous consumers were held hostage to the gouging prices.

I rode my bike each day, a ferry familiar route I had taken during the Naomi times. I saved fifty dollars to buy a '64 Ford Falcon, which could be started with a screwdriver. After two days and the ink yet to dry on the bill of sale, someone discovered the trick, and the Falcon flew away during the night. This driver was screwed.

"Stole your car? That's just a damn excuse!" my new boss said. The offshore equipment owner handed me a pink slip.

As heartless as he was, he was right. I knew I had answers but did not act upon them—call the boss, ride a bike, ask for a ride, hitchhike, jog, or catch the city bus. Any of these would have been more productive than wasting energy brewing about a car I'd never see again. In time, I leaned on prior experience. I used the jobs as motivation to where I wanted to go and to what I wanted to achieve. I had slowly become better at standing, moving, and surviving everything but one—Naomi. She was the hardest habit to break, a reality I could neither accept nor love.

At every turn of a street corner or streetcar, park, body of water, school, burger dive, Montego or FIAT, I saw Naomi's face. And heard her voice—a whisper in the wind blowing in my ears, which had blown a hurricane upon my heart. I watched lovers love, ride bikes, hold hands, and exchange forever vows. Loneliness pushed me into a hole of isolation and darkness, until I dug my way out, only to fall in again. The emotional and economical roller coaster reminded me of Uncle Clay's binge drinking.

But Uncle Clay once told me that "the sun doesn't shine on the same dog's ass every day, but if it shines on you, take advantage of it." I did. The clouds parted ways to let the rays through, just enough to purchase my oldest brother's '72 blue body, white hardtop, Chevy Monte Carlo. The sale price, like the Falcon, was a steal, but unlike the Ford, the General Motor required keys to start the engine. I secretly dubbed it the "Montego" Carlo, but "The Blue Blur" had become its immortalized name, since it had once spent numerous nights streaking from the French Quarter to the lakefront—burning a hole in the *Best of '67* eight track.

While I was grateful for *The Blur*, I had moved financially further into the red, the color of cash I despised. Only one quarter of the money needed to attend Ole Miss was sitting in my savings account. Life's internal clock was ticking—fall further behind my peers and wait to return to Oxford or enroll at a more affordable in-state school? This meant staying stuck in Louisiana, which meant loving reality, which meant bartender give me a beer. Maybe two. Enter SLU.

Hammond resided an hour from Gretna and had been a flyby when traveling in the 280Z. On slower Amtrak and Greyhound trips I had used as alternate transportation, I could feel from the window its small-town appeal. When riders exited and boarded, I observed locals sauntering about trying to get nowhere fast.

But I had known nothing about Southeastern Louisiana University, save for its LSU similar letters and a coach named Brewer—an ex-Ole Miss football player. Word on the street said that he was hard-nosed but fair. His alma mater had given me second thoughts about "walking on," as I walked around the SLU campus, then released the notion into the August light.

The more I roamed, the more I *knew something* was missing. The plethora of pine trees and flat terrain left me longing for Oxford's rolling hills, the smell of football, and walks through Faulkner's woods. The feeling intensified after I unloaded *The Blue Blur* and checked into a dorm of bunkbeds and community showers—poles apart from the luxuries of Hilton on the Hill. I had to remind myself where I had come from. And in that moment, it wasn't New Orleans.

The next morning, I went to a required zoology class and discovered it had nothing to do with animals and everything to do with a complicated plant system. I left to go change my class schedule, but not before a student informed me that zoology was across the hall from botany. I didn't change my schedule; I changed my mind and headed home.

*****

"Just didn't feel right." I tried explaining the inexplicable to my parents—why after two days I had left Hammond. "I was going to change my schedule but went to withdraw instead. Something in the deepest part of me said it has to be Ole Miss." It was another way of saying I had to change my environment. And create more miles between my memory and Naomi.

My desire for her was only matched by my desire to return to Oxford. But this was a controlled passion, driven by a purpose to run to something and to run from her shadow and her skin which still smothered me. My desire was also driven by the fear of failure and how I could live the life of Uncle Clay and Grandpa Perrett—drink to chase my problem until it catches me. And to share smoking as a common vice, albeit their chosen paper product was tobacco.

Back in Gretna, the job-searching circus started. Again. The lead actor in the sad act was me, a dog chasing its tail. The mind vs. Naomi vs. environment raged on. And the mind vs. the lack of money battle joined the traveling show, and the lack of money was winning. I was financially falling further into the red. By Christmas, I was down and nearly out, a punch-drunk boxer on my knees, the ten-count echoing in my brain. But the blues had taught me that somebody somewhere had it worse, and if they did, I didn't want to know about it.

Though my decadent days and wild ways had receded during the lone Ole Miss semester, there were too many NOLA faces and places to get laid, get high, and suck suds. Too many smiling faces and places of the ghost of Everywhere, Nowhere Naomi. And love was everywhere in the air and nowhere for me. I was only the lonely man—trapped in solitary confinement, a will but no way to escape. My prehospital habits stayed true. Relapse ruled. I settled for polluting my mind and body and one-night stands, which I had gone through at the rate of a pack of chewing gum, but the gum had left a better taste in my mouth.

CHAPTER 21

It had become obvious that my repeated prayers to be taken during the night were left unanswered. But it was not due to a lack of effort, having done what a good Catholic boy had been taught to do. I followed their God lines and checked the Catholic Cannons handed down by the sixteenth century Council of Trent. I also reviewed my checklist: rosary under the pillow, a holy water bottle, unlit bedside candle, and a fourth-grade confirmation scapula. Desperate prayers called for desperate measures, enough hocus pocus and *Hoc est corpus meum* to propel me past St. Peter's pearly gates at the speed of light. Nothing worked.

Maybe the whispering voice, which guided me many years ago, was telling me to stick around, plenty of life had yet been lived. But each day, I awoke with a paralyzing possibility that my goal to coach was a fabrication by a simple-minded boy who should accept his place in Gretna's society. Doubt ruled the day and had given me cause to consider capitulation—find a job, find a girl, find or make a family, and find forty years down the road I had settled for less. Until a divine light had shone a ray of hope upon me.

"Hog?" I asked.

"Zog?" he asked.

"Bro! Where y'at? What's happenin'? Haven't seen you since I left the gates of hell!" Gasoline had spilled down the side of *The Blur*, as I reached to hug Hog, a Shaw summer school cat who ran with the gang after moving into McDonoghville and mooched more than anyone known to man or animal.

"Sho 'nuff, my brudda! Just stopped in here to get me a honey bun. What ya been doin', homey?"

"Just left a honey bun's house, a lovely New Orleans lady who works at Camellia's Grill. Late night munchies?" I asked. I smiled while assuming we had *both* been blowing J's.

"No, no, no," he said. "Can't do da Mary Jane shit no mo. Not fo a while at least."

"Can't or don't want to? Some days, I'd like to quit," I said.

"Can't, man. I joined da military. They will drug test yo ass."

"You're in the military?"

"Air National Guard. I'm a Food Service Specialist," he said.

"Food Service Specialist?"

"That, sir, is big time for cook," he said.

"Weekend warrior! You like it?"

"Man, I love it, bra. One weekend a month and two weeks in da summa."

"You need a ride home?" I asked. Hog jumped in and provided more military details. "Why did you join? And why be a cook?"

"Bra, cook is da best damn job in da Guard. You go in early and you leave early. And it's easy. And nobody, and I mean nobody messes with the mess hall. Dem cats love to eat. But da number one reason I joined 'cause da military pays college tuition," he said.

"What? They pay your tuition?"

"In-state. And pay fo everything. Books, too. And I'm learning a trade."

"Sounds like a damn commercial. How'd you get this smart?" I asked.

"Man, get outta here," Hog said. "Truth is, a friend of mine told me about it. And no way in hell my folks sendin' my black ass to college."

"Mine aren't sending this white trash, either." I lost sight of him when he eclipsed the front porch. I wondered why people hated because of skin color. I cranked the car and drove to a porch just as small and dark, replayed our talk and thought perhaps a prayer had been answered.

*****

"This is how I see it, Pop," I said. We delved into deviled eggs and red beans and rice. "I have to crap or get off the pot. I'll be twenty-four in March with nothing to show for it except one college semester, too many worthless jobs, and just as many women. I need some structure and a challenge, something that will build my confidence. The Guard will pay for my college tuition, too. If college doesn't work out, I'll at least have a trade."

The conversation with Hog enlightened me to possibilities and reenergized my goal to coach, a goal which nearly evaporated into another "Naomi what might have been"—and having to live with the anguish of never recapturing missed opportunities. The conversation I had with my Air Guard recruiter was sealed with a promise and a path which could one day get me on an athletic field.

"Sounds like you've been thinking about it," my dad said. He opened a cold beer, much to the distaste of my mom who grumbled until he finished it.

"There's only one hitch. It must be the Louisiana Guard."

"What do you want to do while you're in it?"

"Jet Engine Mechanic. Figure if I'm in the Air Force, then I may as well learn about planes. I imagine there's nothing better than a good plane and nothing worse than a bad one. Kind of like a marriage," I said. "Can't be a pilot. That requires a college degree. Hell, I'm struggling just to get off the ground."

"That makes sense," he said. "Jet Engine Mechanic pays good money, too, Roux. Those jobs will be around as long as planes keep flying." Although my parents could be hardheaded, I always held an admiration for what they endured. From family alcoholism to war, death scratched on their windowpanes. Living with them made money saving sense, but I frequently felt I was a financial burden. But they never stated anything to the contrary.

"Yep, but you know I want to coach. It's in me, and it's got to come out," I said. I didn't have the heart to tell him my desire to be a mechanic was on par with being a cook. Neither quaked my occupational soul.

"Well, do what makes you happy, 'cause ya gotta do it every damn day," he said. I noticed grease under his fingernails, and while I loved getting my hands dirty, my dirt resided on a ball field, outside in the elements where blood and sweat fertilized the grass.

I thought about the conversation I had with my dad on my return home from the Air Guard base. And I thought how I'd explain to him what had transpired during the swearing-in ceremony. In less than a minute, I had given my oath to fulfill four years with Uncle Sam. A colonel commanded me to "raise your right hand and repeat after me."

"So, how did it go, military man?" my dad asked. He had a bright gleam in his eye as he arrived home from work. It crossed my mind to ask if he had to clear the ferry railing.

"Not the best birthday, popper-stopper. The recruiter trapped me. He said the only Jet Engine Mechanic opening was a year away, and the only thing available was a Food Service Specialist, which is far less appetizing."

"A what?"

"A cook! I can't wait a year. Time's not on my side. I had to decide right then and there." I had been forewarned about recruiters who spoke out both sides of their mouths. Mine had put me on the spot, asking me to commit while he reneged on his. I wondered if he had a daughter named Naomi.

"Shit. So, what did you tell them?" he asked. I decided to trust my instincts and join for the tuition only, and only for a year, before I'd transfer across the state line.

"I solemnly swear to support and defend…" My right hand raised, and the fingers on my left hand crossed, casually hidden behind my back—the same two fingers I had crossed years prior when I confessed about the condom box.

*****

Six weeks of basic training was like a bad song—hard to listen to and harder to get out of my head. And it seemed to have received airman airplay at every turn of the dial. I had been surrounded by souls deprived of jambalaya, crawfish pie, and filet gumbo. It made me miss my Mississippi River and my Mississippi Oxford at dusk, when the evening sunlight silenced time.

And I thirsted for the taste of human touch. Since Naomi, I longed uncontrollably to visit that well. I sometimes took solace in the female DI, Sergeant Blue Eyes, who partnered as our marching commander and inquired, "Why do you always smile when I give an order," as she wore a smile on her face, all the way to the end of week six.

By graduation day, our lead DI proclaimed our squadron to have been the worst marching group to pass through Lackland—validated in my *Basic Training* book with the inscription: "Herzog, the worst squad leader in Air Force history. And the ugliest, too. Good luck at Lowry. You'll need it." I took it all as a compliment. As Lagniappe, Sergeant Blue Eyes wrote her home phone number and address, which I read at thirty thousand feet, flying to tech school in Denver on a rocky mountain high, a Texas size smile on my face.

*****

On December 8 at 5:00 p.m., the *Sunset Limited* headed west out of the New Orleans Union Passenger Terminal. I skimmed through my *Basic Training* book and reminisced about tech school and how a Colorado snow had fallen for the first time on my final day at Lowery Air Force Base. The weather's *Auld Lang Syne* bid me farewell, sending me home as an official Food Service Specialist. The book and my diploma blanketed me, as the train traveled atop the Huey Long Bridge, cast iron dangling on a precipice, human flesh hanging in the balance.

Secretly stashed under the book were letters and a *Playboy* magazine. I had grown from a picture-gawking stage to a fondness for the more tasteful interviews. Friends chided me when I shared this, stating that the literature was a ruse. December's article had taught me more about John Lennon than I could have imagined. Immersed in the transcript, Baton Rouge and Lafayette had passed me by.

I had closed my eyes and hummed "While My Guitar Gently Weeps," recounting the times David, Billy, Perry, Ray, and I joy rode every inch of The Big Sleazy, smoking herb while burning a hole in the White Album—white birds singing in the dead of night, teenage tears in my eyes thinking of Naomi.

"San Antonio! San Antonio! Next stop, San Antonio!" the conductor announced.

Miss Blonde Hair, Blue-Eyed Drill Instructor appeared in an early morning mist, calling out my name in a voice much softer than I had known during boot camp. "You made it!"

"Yes, me and the letters you wrote." Letters which had more sexual overtones than a *Playboy* magazine. "I took a nap on the train. Just for you."

"Thank you, Airman."

"May I turn on the radio?" I asked. We drove through the fog in her beat-up Pinto. "I learned as a teenager that music helps stimulate the mood." I searched for a Beaker Street sound, until only the news came clean: "Last night on his way to a studio session, John Lennon was shot and killed…"

My mind swam to the beat of driftwood riding the river current. Lennon's death was another reminder that I was a whisper in the wind, which could be blown away without a warning—magnified by the fact that I had been reading the interview during the time he was murdered. The shock and timing sent chills across my body during the long return ride to the Crescent City. It reopened the memories of Ray's brother who'd been fatally shot while sitting in a work van, an empty wallet on the floor. And the day a distant cousin lost his balance and his life, accidentally shooting himself with a .357 Magnum.

I also thought of my ability to land in precarious positions, then drown in its absurdity, as though the Naomi relationship had taught me nothing. Or perhaps it taught all the wrong things, and I was powerless to walk away, simply because the chase game was too intriguing. Why would I travel ten hours just to sleep with my drill instructor, who unbeknownst, had a child for me to babysit when she went to bark marching orders and perhaps catch more suitors on the base? One of which, who had discovered that two days with a two-year-old was the ultimate eye-opener.

"Sorry. My mom's been hospitalized, and I need to get home," I told her. One hand had held my suitcase, with two fingers crossed.

"Oh, I'm sorry, too. I wish you could have stayed longer," she said. One hand had held her two-year-old.

While bad habits followed me everywhere, and I was insanely glad to take them with me, four months away equipped me with a cleaner pair of eyes, which led me to believe I could make college happen at home in spite of the Hammond debacle. Besides, I had been locked into a quasi-commitment with the Louisiana Air Guard. Enter LSU.

A month after I hung my military fatigues in my parent's house, I enrolled tuition free and parked the car in front of a dorm off Dalrymple Drive in Baton Rouge. During a January rain, I hauled my clothes up to floor eight, laid in bed, and stared at the ceiling. The horrible, Hammond hurricane of doubt and nearby Naomi waged war. My gut was screaming. And it had my attention.

"You're in the wrong place at the wrong time," Gut said. "You only *think* you *want* to be here, but you *know* where you *need* to be.

And Naomi is just down the road. Sooner or later, *you will* contact her."

"Crazy, huh?" I asked the dorm director after my gut kicked my butt to reload the car. Mr. Monitor gave me a long look, like I should perhaps check into a psych ward. "At least I didn't jump from the eighth floor. And by the way, one day, I'm gonna run a dorm." He was probably thankful it was not the one who employed him. The rain had ceased when I stepped into the Louisiana light. Homeward bound.

"Just didn't feel right?" my dad asked. Sarcasm was a Herzog trait.

"I love LSU. It'll always be a part of me, but I will not be able to study there. Something keeps telling me to return to Ole Miss. It feels like I'd rather die of thirst in Oxford than drown in drunkenness in Baton Rouge." I bowed my head, as though I had let them down, again, the prodigal son.

"Jesus, Richard. You didn't give it a chance," my mom said.

"I have to do this on my terms, down my road, no matter how long it takes. Sometimes, y'all, a person must listen to his instincts. Even though most of my 'ins' stink."

CHAPTER 22

"I would like to introduce Richard Herzog as a graduate assistant to our staff," Coach Brewer said. The year was 1984. The former USL coach had his Ole Miss head football coach arm wrapped around my 4.0 GPA undergraduate shoulder. By the time I had left Oxford in '79 and returned in '81, he had worked his way up the crazy college coaching ladder and returned to our alma mater in 1983. "Richard's come a long way. He remembered when I was in Hammond, and our roads came together."

"Sirs," I said. I nodded and tried to breathe. We stood before a table in the War Room, while his staff stared at a skinny Cajun kid who knew little about the intricacies of college football.

"He'll run the athletic dorm and assist Coach S with the quarterbacks," Coach Brewer said. The words flashed the face of the LSU dorm monitor, his incredulous, wide eyes and his mouth agape. He would have thought Coach Brewer insane to have hired me.

But there I stood in a humble stance, feeling prophetic, a plethora of jobs and two Louisiana universities behind me, New Orleans in the rearview mirror, a silhouette of Naomi in the back seat. She still rode in the ride of my mind, as I scratched and crawled my way back to North Mississippi. Naomi had walked in my memory the day I entered the First National Bank and secured a ten-thousand-dollar school loan at 9 percent interest. She had walked in my skin the day I transferred to the Mississippi National Guard, much to the chagrin of the Louisiana unit. The bank loan and the Guard gave me the money; Naomi provided the incentive. I learned to walk when I was injured; no amount of her pain could keep me down. But I could never figure out a way to shake the habits she brought with me.

And there I stood, in front of a dozen SEC coaches, feeling badly for fired Coach L, the first college coach I had met when I first entered Hilton on the Hill. He was kind enough to let me room with John F when I returned to Ole Miss after a two-year hiatus. But the staff he was on didn't win enough games. It must have been hard on him and his family to have been shown the dormitory door I occupationally inherited. Money mattered at the golden gates of Southeastern Conference Football. Win and the bucks flow in. Lose and the bucks run out. And so do the coaches.

*****

"They were right to give it to you. I had the dorm title when the new staff was hired, but you did most of the work the last three years, but nobody knew about it," Jern said. He was the first graduate assistant I had searched for, after being introduced in the War Room. "The letter you wrote to Coach S must have helped."

From '81 through '84, I did the behind the scenes grunt work, even during the time of Coach Brewer's announcement. It was the most thankless job I had experienced. The thought I had many years prior with Coach L came back to haunt me. *It was beyond comprehension why anyone could or would run an athletic dorm.* But I was determined to find or make a way to earn a diploma and to coach, including walking the halls at 1:00 a.m. while reading Faulkner novels. My desire to accomplish, along with my fear of failure, were only surpassed by the shadow of Naomi, which had cast itself in a castle filled with male athletes. Each day, I placed one foot at a time onto the floor, and each day was a grind to get beyond her.

"I had much practice writing in high school. My freshman English teacher pushed me. She was very persuasive," I said.

"Must have been a good teacher," he said.

"She was good in a number of ways," I said. I watched him and the other GA's breakdown sixteen-millimeter football film.

"You know what GA stands for?" Danny asked. He had white hair and whiter skin and played linebacker for the previous staff. "Go for assistant. Go for this, go for that," he said. He looked none the happier for the task at hand.

"Good one, but I don't care if it stands for glorified asshole," I said. "They're paying for my grad school, room, and board, and cut me a check for two hundred a month. If they tell me to go scrub toilets with a toothbrush, I will. And I'll bring the toothpaste. Hell, I did that in boot camp."

I was quick to remember how each penny had counted during the spring of '79, when I walked every other Friday with energetic anticipation to my mailbox at the student union. That was "when the eagle flew"—payday. And I had flown to the Bursar's office to cash the ten-dollar check my mother sent. Ten felt like a hundred to an old freshman. I could not thank her enough, nor could I escape the guilt for taking their money when they had little to give.

"You were in the military?" Danny asked.

"Still am. I have a few more weekend drills. My four years are about up, and it helped pay my undergrad tuition."

"Man, how old are you?" asked Tony, one of Coach Brewer's linebackers at La Tech.

"Twenty-seven."

"Damn. How old were you when you started college?" curly hair Skip asked. He and Tony had tobacco chew between their gums and spit cups on a table.

"Twenty-three." I skipped the details.

Later that night, I leaned against the dorm wall, rehashing the news of the day while remembering where I had come from. I reflected on the pure joy and fact that college at Ole Miss was everything I knew it could be, because I made it everything it would be. I thought about how I had used hard times to propel me forward, to never waste a day, even though scars remained.

While there existed a cornucopia of coeds who resided hip to hip with me in the Blue Blur, Naomi had two, steady hands on my steering wheel. My dependence on romantic love or the destructive myth of the "feeling of falling in love" was a daily presence; I embraced it with the same veracity as academics, the dorm, exercising, and eating.

A case in point was Liza, who had driven a 1980, two-door Mustang with a Lauderdale County license plate. But when we were together, I did most of the driving—in her cramped, rear seat. We had discovered all the secluded spots Ole Miss offered; and we created three of our own. The woodpecker, which had hammered back in the Naomi days, had nothing on us. And our Liza love sessions lasted until sweat saturated the cloth covering, and she had claimed to love me like no other.

After three months of passionate "dating," holding hands, and sharing food at the University Commons and thinking I had a college girlfriend, I asked her to my first Ole Miss Homecoming football game. Like the gentleman I had professed to be, I arrived at her dorm at noon for a 1:00 p.m. kickoff. My brother, David, who had made his first campus visit, came along. He and I sat on the steps awaiting Mona Liza to descend from her third-floor room, when a younger man approached from the parking lot.

We stared at the grass and the October clouds until she arrived, and I had introduced her to my brother. She in turn politely introduced us to her boyfriend. "We've been dating since high school," she said. Her Meridian drawl had washed over the wave of incredulousness, which washed over me.

"Your who?" David asked.

"My boyfriend." I figured Ms. Cat had decided to play while Mr. Mouse was away—another Naomi act-alike.

"Well," I said to her boyfriend, "I'd like you to meet my girlfriend who I've been fucking hard and heavy since the semester began." David and I headed to the stadium.

Three hours after the football game, I committed to the duplicitous team. For my remaining Ole Miss tenure, I played Mr. Mouse while my Ms. Pussycats were away or asleep in their dorm rooms or apartments. Thereafter, the only medicine which diverted my eyes and my mind from coeds was a whistle and a football.

*****

A million miles of minutes had passed—a leather ball spiraled through four football seasons, around and around, a continuous carousel. Prudence was hard to find. College had come and gone, and I had carried coaching confidence into the real world, thinking I could break any chain which bound me. A coach's life had occupied more time than a day gave—meetings, game planning, practices, games, grading game film, film of the next opponent, field work, strength and conditioning, fundraising, equipment, banquets, putting out fires, parents, teaching, Booster Club—and marriage.

Four years from Ole Miss and having coached at a small high school in Jackson, Mississippi, my wife and I moved our belongings and our cat, Gumbo, to Nashville. I thought a change of state and scenery would eventually erase Naomi, especially since I accepted a GA position with Vanderbilt Football. I hopped back into the crazy college coaching world, jumping from a small pan and back into the large SEC fire.

I was wrong. Though I worked more hours than a lawyer, I could not shake the daily demon who visited during the darkest recesses or whenever a good-looking lady appeared on my radar—the call to chase, capture, and release those things which were forbidden. To worsen matters, I occasionally read a Naomi letter, a medicinal cure every bit as potent as pot and alcohol.

But the medicine was akin to insanity, knowing I had grown beaten down by a past which I could never escape, while having letters and songs which helped me to remember. Fifteen plus years had passed, and I'd become a weary coach who preached toughness but was too soft to wash her from my skin. At best, I wanted kids to avoid what I experienced. At worst, I had a difficult time helping myself. I had no certainty to what continued to cause the lust, lies, and liquor. Terminal conflict. Enter the therapists.

"Let me get this straight," said one of many and my least favorite. "Are you saying you want to die?" He was a squatty, middle-aged man who had difficulty walking.

"No. What I'm saying is that at times I don't want to live anymore. I learned this from my mother. Do you understand the difference between the two?" I asked.

"I do not see a difference. If you're saying you no longer want to live, then I see that as a threat to harm yourself. Which, in that case, I have to contact the police."

"What?"

"I'll have to call the police. You are threatening to commit suicide. As a professional therapist, I'm obligated to call."

"I didn't say I wanted to kill myself! And why in the hell am I here if I can't express how I feel? You can call anybody you want! I'm leaving!"

"If you leave, I'll still call, and sooner or later, they *will* find you and take you to the emergency room. So, shall I call?" he asked. "Or, I can call your wife, and she can take you."

"No! Do not call her! We're separated."

"Then who should I call if not the police?"

"I believe it's 'whom' should I call?"

"Okay, I'll call the law!" His tone insinuated he had grown impatient with his smart-ass patient, which was okay with me. I had grown tired of my crazy-ass self speaking to a nutcase.

"Call my principal where I coach. He'll come get me," I said.

*****

Twenty-one years after my twenty-first birthday, there it was—Emergency. A sign flashed its neon red against a blue dusk at Vanderbilt Medical Center. The shame I felt being dropped off a few doors down from my wife's place of employment was embarrassing and frightening.

Abashed. Apologetic. Again. Afraid to speak. I sunk in the front seat of Principal Jim's truck and covered my face. He asked no questions but showed concern that one of his coaches was supposedly threatening to end his life. He was one of the few administrators whom I could confide in and trust.

"I'm haunted by an experience I had in high school. I've never been able to shake it or deal with it in a positive way," I said.

The emergency room gurney was surrounded by green curtains, and I was turning blue from the frigid room temperature. I longed for the wall heater I stood against on many McDonoghville mornings, trying to understand why Naomi ended our relationship. Jim's eyes shifted from the cold floor to my colder eyes. "Do what you need to do. I'll get you a substitute, if you need one. Just get yourself better." Security—just what the doctor ordered. "Have you called home?"

"No. Would you..."

"I will. I know things have not been well for y'all," he said.

"Thank you. Did I tell you that I had a therapist tell me that I was lucky to be alive?" I asked.

"No."

"And one night, I was standing in the Gin, a bar in Oxford, and the athletic director said I could be described in one word: 'survivor'."

"I can tell that by your work ethic," he said. I wasn't sure why I was telling him these things; I guess I wanted him to know that I was not permanently insane but temporarily wounded.

The ER doctor decided I presented no harm to myself nor to anyone else. He spoke briefly about suicide protocol, then ordered another round of evaluations by experts stationed a block away. I was not too psychotic to believe that the health care system was a brotherhood, pushing people down an assembly line of tests and drugs, causing folks to become gravely ill once they received their medical bills. Jim wished me the best and gave me a hug instead of an administrative handshake.

"You can go get clothes and toiletries, but you have an hour to return or the men in blue *will* come after you," said the VU Psych Center receptionist. Checkpoint Charlie sat too wide for his chair and too underworked for what they were undoubtedly overpaying him. He issued a key and a room number, reminding me of my Ole Miss dorm days. I wondered if the athletes had seen me as Checkpoint Charlie, too thin to look like a coach, an overworked and underpaid grad assistant.

I returned from my apartment to a dimly lit room that was colder than the E.R. The floor pained my knees, as I gave praying another shot. No checklist. No rosary. No holy water. No candle. No saints, priests, or nuns. Just simple words dispatched to an empyreal deity I'd never seen but had been preached to believe in the certainty of his existence.

What sleep I slept was spent in a nightmare, a Frankenstein fellow fit me into a straitjacket, when a tap and a voice at the door awakened me. Thirty minutes to be ready for the day—breakfast, one-on-one counseling, and group therapy for the "real sick" people. Five miles away my family slept, clueless that I was a thousand miles afar, adrift on an island. By the day's end, I had returned to my room, looking through a window at autumn's last leaves, when I was summoned to the counselor's office.

"Mr. Herzog, we are releasing you, but we recommend that you contact this professional, who'll encourage you to take a test. She's highly qualified. I'll fax her our notes and your history and discuss what has happened here," said the counselor.

"Can y'all pinpoint the problem?" I asked.

"Not to undermine or underestimate your struggles, but your issue is more trauma based as the result of a past event. Our expertise deals in mental issues ranging from anorexia nervosa to schizophrenia. But there is a good chance she can help." I wanted to ask if I qualified as a schizophrenic, since I could daily hear Naomi's voice inside my head. I declined, fearing it would spark another round of testing.

"Ma'am, I have tried since 1975 to find out what's wrong with me. Most days, I didn't know if I was running against the wind or chasing after it. And here we are in 2000 and you know someone who can not only tell me but help me?" I asked.

"It's worth a try."

"Thank you."

As I walked away, I took hope in the possibility of answers, since I had lived alone and in the constant state of fear. The torment of being separated from my family far exceeded the pain of being without Naomi. Of the two, one was physically gone; the other had a chance. I had to find or make a way which transcended the drive and energy it had taken to become a coach. Failing in marriage and not daily seeing our children grow up was a recipe for suicide.

Loneliness smothered me when I returned to grab my scant belongings from the room. But I acknowledged a crease of light which had shone through my dirty window—even in the cold confines of a psych facility.

*****

One hundred questions. A real ACT exam—forthright, objective, and exposing—peeling skin layers which had hidden lurid, shady secrets from the past to the present. Here I was, once again testing like my life or career depended on it. I carefully bubbled the ovals, humming "Ninety-Nine Bottles of Beer on the Wall," while sitting on a deck under a maple tree. No guessing. No second-guessing. I had to answer the questions truthfully or continue down a deadly decline.

"I must admit that I've never dreaded something so much that I've looked so forward to," I said.

"Well, Richard, there is nothing more sobering than discovering your problems and nothing more liberating, either," said Ms. K, an addiction evaluation specialist. "You scored a ninety-five, a high grade with serious news. But there are solutions."

"I'm listening," I said.

My head and the song still hummed an hour after I had finished the test. "You are a classic codependent with an insatiable desire to love and be loved. Your insecurity is off the charts. Most revealing is that you are obsessed with being in a secretive relationship or in a relationship where more than one person is involved. You're equally enamored with the chase, the hunt, but once you get what you want, you're ready to move on. You probably learned this from the schoolteacher, but you were the prey and she was the predator. Your family history of depression only complicates the matter."

"If she's a predator, does this mean she never truly loved me?" I asked.

"She was in a position of authority and power, and she misused both. Teenagers are vulnerable and can be easily manipulated. Without personally knowing her, I can't say whether she loved you are not, but the fact remains, she abused her position as a teacher. In my opinion, you were far too young to handle the situation, especially considering the environment in which you were raised. No child should experience what you did, but it happens. And it happens mostly with a male teacher and a female student," she said. "Rarely the other way around. Unfortunately, the maimed often has addict tendencies, be it alcohol, drugs, or sex. Name it. Addicts use some sort of medicine to pacify rooted trauma," she said.

"I wish I could say you were wrong," I said. The revelation was another streetcar moment. I had believed that my time with Naomi was real and true, and she had filled my biggest void—love. Now I had to determine if she truly loved me or if she abused me. "This is a lot to absorb, maybe too much. *Jesus.* All these years, I have searched for an answer and a way to fix it. How do I handle this?"

"Well, like I said, 'There are solutions.' You need to take medicine, which doesn't require a pill or drinking or smoking or fornicating—medicine that will work. I have a suggestion where to start, but it's going to take time and work ethic on your part," she said.

"Work is something I've always embraced. I know how to roll up my sleeves," I said. Her words felt like I had scored six points, the feeling a football player gets when he lands into pay dirt.

"Good. But you must be patient. And most of all, you must take one step at a time."

More like twelve steps at a time.

DECEMBER 21, 2000

"It grew into something which nearly killed me, more than once, actually" I said. The Joey K server refilled my water glass. Sheets of rain pelted the windows.

"How?"

"It was more of a matter of *why* than *how*."

"Okay. I meant how did that happen and why?"

"*Why* is easy to answer. It was impossible to move past you. *How* was just a method. The thought had been planted, when I saw a man jump from the bridge. I was a child."

"I remember you telling me that a long time ago," she said.

"A long time ago with us is like yesterday. The good and the bad thoughts never go away. I planned to jump from the bridge the night of a concert. And strange as it may sound, the show saved me. It was an epiphany."

"You said there was more than one."

"Yes, but the second was not purposely planned. I drank a fifth of Bacardi the night I turned twenty-one. I ended up in the hospital for five days."

"What was it?" she asked.

"Alcohol poisoning. One thing about being in a hospital bed, alone, looking at the night…"

"What?"

"It gave me time to think about the missed athletic opportunities. And how our relationship set me back years behind my peers. I realized how you stole a pivotal part of my childhood. You introduced me to adulthood long before it was time. It's a scar I might carry for life."

Naomi had her familiar, faraway look, staring beyond the windshield I'd seen a hundred times while sitting in the Montego and the FIAT. The same gaze she had when she refused to answer my before and after streetcar questions.

"Were you working at the time?" she asked. She remained good at changing the conversational direction.

"Yes. I was a meter reader for the Gas Company. One of *many* jobs. What about you?" I asked.

"I guess I was still at Shaw or teaching at Holy Cross College. You said many jobs. What others?"

"Let's just say that I had become quite skilled at finding a job and more skilled at quitting to find another. Twenty or more, perhaps. Everything but sniffing farts on auto seats at a car wash. I was so fucked up when I left Shaw. I had a boatload of bad habits and a shitload of dirty laundry and no way to clean either one of them."

"Well, that's interesting…"

"No, that's sad…"

"I meant the part about the car wash." She managed a smile but couldn't manage to eat her food, while I managed to eat without smiling. "But you were not always in those jobs. I ran into your brother, and he said you had become a successful coach," she said.

"Yes. Long story but not as long as it took to get there."

"I'm listening."

"It goes back to the hospital. God gave me another chance. I decided I was going to coach because it *was the only thing* I knew. And *nothing*, not even your ghost was going to stop me."

"But that would have required college."

I described *how* and *why* I attended Shaw football games after I had graduated. I included a terse depiction of my disposition each time I left the contests, and *how* and *why* it added more fuel to my desire to coach.

"So, where did you go to college?" she asked.

"Ole Miss."

"My son went there for a semester but didn't like it. He said it was…different. I drove him up there. It's a pretty campus." The thought of *her* son at *my* college was too shocking. I excused myself to the restroom.

When I reached the stall, I silently screamed my mom's goddamnsonofabitchandbastard, while I threw punches at the air. I thought about the therapist who strongly advised against meeting with her. In a louder muted voice I said, *Screw him! The only way to move forward is to stand in the fire—the same way I stood in the stadium agonizingly watching Shaw football games—where fire had transformed to desire and placed me on the road to coaching.*

"Ole Miss, huh?" I asked as I returned.

"Yes, how did you end up going there? It's so far away."

I explained how I got to see the university. A change of culture was another, indispensable reason why. New memories and footprints had called. I either left NOLA or I'd die young. "There you go."

"Wait. That doesn't tell me how you became a coach," she said.

"Why is that important?"

"Well, my second husband is a coach and…"

"I really don't care what he does or what he did. I have no interest in a person you lied about marrying. Especially, when you were supposed to marry me. Do you remember what I asked you and what you told me three days before my senior year ended when you were driving me home?"

"Can't say that I do."

"I asked if you were remarrying. That was the word around campus. You said, 'I wish someone would send me an invitation, because it's news to me. I promise.' Like an idiot, I believed you, even when I knew you were lying when you *promised.* You were good at making promises and better at breaking them. Two months later, I heard you were married. It was devastating." I wanted to include the list of excuses of why she had probably married him but set it aside for a possible future date.

"I guess I was scared to tell you. I was a big chicken."

"It was probably best that you lied. No telling what I would've done. Maybe that's one of the reasons a therapist told me that I was lucky to be alive. I agreed and told him there were others who were just as lucky to be alive," I said. Water formed in my eyes.

"You saw a therapist?"

"Therapists. Plural. I ended with a counselor who sent me to take a written test for 'trauma-based' clients. You were the trauma, and I was the base."

"A written test?"

"Yep. Just like an English multiple choice, and I scored a high grade." The Joey K server arrived and asked if everything was okay with the food. "I took the test the day after I was served divorce papers." I sat, staring into her space.

"And?"

"And I told him that I didn't believe in divorce, and that I'd never sign those papers. God didn't place me in Nashville to see my marriage fail. He placed me there to save it," I said.

"Well, you've always been strong-willed."

"Had to be." I detailed the long, winding road—from my first Ole Miss semester until the day I was awarded the GA position— finally answering her question as to how I had become a coach.

"That is a long road," she said.

"Can you imagine? A kid who missed high school football and ends up on a SEC staff? And that wasn't the only one. After coaching at a high school in Jackson, Mississippi, my mentor invited me to be a grad assistant at Vanderbilt."

"You went to school there?"

"Yes, but the most important test I had taken was the one we just talked about—the written one which landed me in a twelve-step program. You see, what was far worse than the alcohol and the drugs, more venomous, were the women. What I learned from you was how to chase and release. To play the duplicitous game. It was deeply ingrained in me. It's what I learned from our relationship. Lust and lie. And it took twenty-five years to land in a place where I got answers, and the answers allowed me to be with my wife and family."

"How long have you been in twelve-steps?"

"A month. Hard and heavy. It's been the closest I've come to church in a long time. I learned rest would only come when I'd let go and let God. I learned that my past didn't have to be my future, and the pain doesn't have to last."

"Well, if it helps. I recently had an affair with a man," Naomi admitted. She brushed lint from her tight sweater, which matched a hint of grey splendor in her hair.

"As opposed to a woman? No, it doesn't help, nor does it surprise me. But I'm not throwing stones." I glanced at my watch. Three hours had passed. I had learned to be mindful of time, since I had lost years of it.

"I wish there were something I could say," she said.

"Speaking of saying. Have you told anybody about us?" I asked.

"No."

"Absolutely nobody?"

"Not one person. I would have lost everything."

"*You! You* would have lost everything? *I* almost lost everything to your nothing! My marriage. My children. High school sports. My soul," I said.

"I don't know what to say other than I'm sorry."

"For years, all I've heard is how girls are victims of male teachers. How women are exploited and sexually abused. Well, it happened to people like me, too. A male. I grew up in a culture where a boy should boast about his sexual accomplishments—as though it's a game. When love and sex are combined, the lines on the game field get blurred. And it feels more like exploitation, and that has no gender."

"I wasn't exploiting you. I was just doing what I wanted to do at the time," she said.

"So, it was about your own selfish desire..."

"No."

"I was left to sink or swim, and you? You only had to hide," I said. "But I sought *you*, because I know *you* would *never* seek me. And I sought you because I am supposed to forgive you. And that's so damn hard."

"Yes, I've been hiding," she said. The rain had stopped, and the sun winked through the clouds. All the searching and suffering and sex and drinking and drugs had fallen upon me in one single shot. I knew in that moment what it meant to survive, and only God, my highest power, rescued me.

"Yes, you have been hiding," I said. Her admission was worth the price of the plane ticket.

A train in the near distance summoned; its whistle whined and called me to the river. I excused myself from the table and grabbed my blue umbrella. And like a thousand times before, I walked south to the Muddy Mississippi and talked to it. And the water clapped its hands.

EPILOGUE

While the terms *child sexual abuse, statutory rape, and statute of limitations,* as they pertain to an adult female and a teenage boy, may have existed during my early high school years, I was unaware of them. Twenty-six years after I graduated, I was informed that Naomi fit the profile of all three. The conflict ensued. Did she sexually abuse me, or did she truly love me?

Statutory rape and *statute of limitations* had become the clearer of the three terms because they were easily definable. *Child sexual abuse,* however, remained nebulous since *abuse* is an umbrella term, which may vary among professional, cultural, and social groups, to list a few. Searching for a concrete answer and coming to terms with this dilemma had taken time. The duration seemed interminable. One of the main reasons it appeared never-ending was because I had continuously lived in denial. I never wanted to accept the fact that I was a victim of her actions. I wanted to believe and wholeheartedly embrace that she loved me, even if a law stated otherwise. After all, love, at that time, was more powerful than flesh. And denial had become more dominant than either.

It was easy for me to accept that everything we did was genuine and unadulterated because we supposedly "loved each other." Furthermore, at that time, it was a modest boost to my teenage self-esteem that a boy as emotionally vulnerable as me could be intimate with an adult in her position. But I never strutted Shaw's High School campus like I was the cock of the walk, an act counter to my guarded disposition.

What helped me reach the decision that Naomi McCarthy Wagenbach sexually molested me? One was the realization that I carried the burden of sexual duplicitousness for most of my life. It was not until I had been tested and entered a twelve-step program that **I realized** I had an incurable urge to catch and release the opposite gender—and more importantly, **I learned** that females were not fish for me to hook any time I wanted to cast a line. An insatiable, habitual need to fall in love metastasized; the results were devastating, destructive, and despicable. I ask God daily for forgiveness, and I thank him for the program which placed me on the path to recovery.

Another factor that helped me reach my decision was the empirical evidence. I learned of and had experienced the repercussions of carnal rape—depression and drug use, anger and violence tendencies, academic and behavioral problems, shame and a destroyed self-esteem, sleepless nights and fatigue-filled days, repeat.

And while I had lived for years in denial, I lived a lifetime of being denied. My entire high school experience amounted to a large empty suitcase—no varsity football, no singularly positive baseball memory, no social clubs, no achievement awards, no plans, no college, no acting, no steady employment, and perhaps, most importantly, no guidance. I barely kept my body and soul intact; suicide was a viable option.

It is my sincere hope that each reader will grasp one of the main purposes of *Pay Dirt:* nonforcible sexual abuse does indeed occur when a female authority figure preys upon a male teenager. And so do the consequences; they are traumatic. For those adolescent boys who have been in similar situations or are currently in it, *there is help. Seek it immediately.* From counseling to telephone hotlines to Child Help Center to the internet—something that never existed when I was a boy. While I can never adequately describe the agony any gender suffers when sexually violated, I can certainly empathize. I can relate to what it is like for a pauper to be crowned king by his fellow high school students. I can relate to promises broken and to the manipulation by an adult who "did what she did because it felt right at the time." I can empathize with the long winding road that led to recovery, and to return to retrieve segments of my soul strewn upon a highway of hell.

With the help from God and my New Orleans resiliency, I endured a tumultuous childhood, a high school hurricane, and years of ceaseless searching. Not only did I endure, but I prevailed. And if I did it, anybody can.

CPSIA information can be obtained
at www.ICGtesting.com
Printed in the USA
LVHW091650190122
708915LV00011B/72